6/98

BUDDHISM
and ZEN

Compiled, Edited, and Translated by
NYOGEN SENZAKI *and*
RUTH STROUT MCCANDLESS

With a foreword by
ROBERT AITKEN

NORTH POINT PRESS

Farrar, Straus and Giroux
New York

North Point Press
A division of Farrar, Straus and Giroux
New York

Contents

Nyogen Senzaki

Nyogen Senzaki was born on the Siberian peninsula of Kamchatka in 1876 of a Japanese mother and an unknown father. He used to joke that he was probably half-Chinese, and indeed he looked rather more Chinese than Japanese. But he himself did not know.

His mother died at his birth, and he was adopted by a Japanese Tendai Buddhist priest who may have been ministering to expatriate Japanese in Siberia. They moved to Japan where the boy grew up and began medical studies, but his education was cut short and his life was completely changed by his adopted father's sudden death. At this tragic loss, young Senzaki renounced the world and became a Zen Buddhist monk, first in the Soto school, then in the Rinzai monastery Enkakuji in Kita Kamakura.

There was no mother figure in young Senzaki's life. He told me that as a boy he tried to visualize the mother who bore him, but could only summon up a vague outline. His adopted father, he said, was an important moral and religious influence:

> My foster father began to teach me Chinese classics when I was five years old. He was a Kegon [Hua-yen] scholar so he naturally gave me training in Buddhism. When I was eighteen years old, I had finished reading the Chinese Tripitaka, but now in this old

age I do not remember what I read. Only his influence remains: to live up to the Buddhist ideals outside of name and fame and to avoid as far as possible the world of loss and gain. [1]

Renouncing the world might have seemed the ultimate fulfillment of his father's teaching, but the young monk found himself in institutional religion, with a hierarchy of titles and authority that was worldly indeed. He loved his teacher, but he came to reject what he called "Cathedral Zen." Reminiscing with his American students some thirty years later, he remarked:

> When my master was alive, I asked him to excuse me from all official ranks and titles of our church, and allow me to walk freely in the streets of the world. I do not wish to be called Reverend, Bishop, or by any other church title. To be a member of the great American people and walk any stage of life as I please, is honorable enough for me. I want to be an American Hotei, a happy Jap in the streets. [2]

Hotei is the so-called Laughing Buddha, a legendary figure who wandered about begging for cakes and fruits, and then gave them to children. When he met monks he would challenge them on a point of realization. "He is my ideal Zen teacher," Senzaki said:

> I do not mean his stoutness, nor his life as a street wanderer, nor his deeds as Santa Claus, but his antichurch idea. Churches are all right as long as they carry the true teaching, but when they start commercializing themselves they spoil the teaching more than anything else. [3]

Senzaki's Zen master was Sōen Shaku, who introduced Zen Buddhism to the United States at the World Parliament of Religions in Chicago in 1893, and who was also a teacher of D. T. Suzuki. He gave Senzaki permission to leave the monastery be-

[1] Nyogen Senzaki, "An Autobiographical Sketch." In Nyogen Senzaki and Ruth Strout McCandless, *The Iron Flute*, p. 161.
[2] Nyogen Senzaki, "On Buddha's Images." In *On Zen Meditation*, p. 99.
[3] Ibid.

fore his formal training was completed, giving him a remarkable "to whom it may concern" letter of approval, dated Autumn, 1901:

> Monk Nyogen tries to live the Bhikku's life according to the teaching of Buddha, to be nonsectarian with no connection to a temple or headquarters; therefore, he keeps no property of his own, refuses to hold a position in the priesthood, and conceals himself from noisy fame and glory. He has, however, the Four Vows— greater than worldly ambition, with Dharma treasures higher than any position, and loving-kindness more valuable than temple treasures.[4]

Senzaki's wanderings took him to northern Japan where he became priest of a little temple and director of its kindergarten. These were perhaps his happiest days. Fifty years after he left Japan for his life in the United States, he was offered a chance to return for a visit. He accepted this invitation largely because he wanted to see the children he had played with in Aomori, some of whom were already grandparents. Those former students who could be reached held a reunion with him, and when he returned to Los Angeles he told us of recognizing them and calling them by name.

His happy days with the children were also days that established his way of teaching. When he set up a Zen center in San Francisco, he called it the *Mentorgarten*, explaining:

> I coined the word "Mentorgarten" as I thought the whole world was a beautiful garden where all friends could associate peacefully, and be mentors of one another. I took the German *garten* instead of "garden" in English, for I was fond of Froebel's theory of kindergarten and thought that we were all children of the Buddha. . . . As in a kindergarten we had no teacher, but we encouraged one another and tried our best to grow up naturally. And like a nurse of the kindergarten, I sometimes presumed myself as a gardener to do all sorts of labor, but I never forgot that I myself

[4]"Sōen Shaku on Nyogen Senzaki" (excerpt). In Nyogen Senzaki and Ruth Strout McCandless, *The Iron Flute*, pp. 159–160.

was also a flower of the garden, mingling with old and new friends. . . . I was always happy in this Mentorgarten, and why will I not be so in the future? This is the . . . spirit of the Sangha in primitive Buddhism, nay, not only in primitive Buddhism, but in modern Buddhism, so far as it is true Buddhism.[5]

The Russo-Japanese war in 1905 interrupted Senzaki's idyll in his garden of children, and he spoke out against it strongly. This was a time of national pride and jingoism, and word of Senzaki's dangerous behavior reached his teacher. What happened next is not clear. Sōen Shaku was invited to San Francisco to give instruction in Zen practice by Mr. and Mrs. Alexander Russell, whom he had met in Chicago in 1893. It may be that he asked Senzaki to join him there, or it may be that Senzaki just showed up. In any case, he appeared and they stayed with their hosts for several months. Then when Sōen Shaku returned to Japan, Senzaki remained in San Francisco.

"Don't try to teach for twenty years," Sōen Shaku advised his student. Senzaki therefore began his American career as a house-boy and a cook, managing his own short-order restaurant for a while. He studied English and Western philosophy diligently, particularly the works of Immanuel Kant. "I like Kant," he once said to me. "All he needed was a good kick in the pants."

Senzaki also taught the Japanese language during this period, and when he saved enough money, he would hire a hall and give a lecture on Buddhism. He took part in various Japanese cultural events as well, and thus gradually established a foundation for his career of teaching Zen.

At last, in 1925, he completed his long apprenticeship, and began teaching in his "floating zendo," meeting in homes and apartments of members. Later, in 1928, with help from friends in Japan as well as in San Francisco, he rented an apartment on

[5]Nyogen Senzaki, "Sangha." In *On Zen Meditation*, p. 69. See Friedrich Froebel, *Pedagogics of the Kindergarten*, trans. by Josephine Jarvis (New York: D. Appleton, 1932).

Bush Street and founded his first center, which was also the first Zen center in the United States.

Though he wanted his students to teach themselves and each other as much as possible, he sought very soon to bring a teacher from Japan to help with their guidance. He was successful in bringing Furukawa Gyōdō Rōshi to San Francisco for a visit, but this was, I gather, a disastrous venture.

Gyōdō Rōshi had been his fellow monk, and was now abbot of Enkakuji, and from the beginning of his visit, he was not amused. Senzaki told me of meeting his ship. There was the rōshi at the rail, resplendent in his robes, and there was Senzaki on the dock, dressed in workpants and a shirt open at the neck. Running along the dock and waving his arms, Senzaki shouted up to his old friend happily, "Dō San!" using the abbreviation of Gyōdō Rō-shi's name that he had always used when they were monks together. It was not the formal greeting that the distinguished rōshi had learned to expect.

There were other unpleasant surprises as well, we can be sure, and before long, the rōshi was on his way back to Japan, and Senzaki then moved to Los Angeles. I have the impression that his move was related to the rōshi's visit, but I don't know the details. In any case, by 1932, Senzaki was living on Turner Street in Los Angeles, alongside the switching yard of the railroad station, the noisiest and dirtiest, and of course the least expensive part of the city.

It was here, in the course of getting acquainted in the Japanese community, that Senzaki met Mrs. Kin Tanahashi, who was to become perhaps his most important friend. Mrs. Tanahashi and her husband had a small business, and she could not afford to hire someone to look after her son, Jimmy, who was mentally disabled. Senzaki offered to care for the boy, and refused any payment. Years later, he told me how much he had enjoyed playing with the child, and what delight it gave him when Jimmy learned to hold his hands palm to palm and say a few syllables of the Four Vows.

Mrs. Tanahashi was deeply impressed by Senzaki, and began Zen study with him. In time, as she prospered as a business-woman, she provided most of his support. The rest of us would leave contributions on his bookshelves, and after the meetings he would go about the room gathering what he called "fallen leaves." If one of the leaves was a twenty-dollar bill, he would carefully put it away "for Shubin San," Mrs. Tanahashi, to help repay her kindness.

It was Mrs. Tanahashi who read an account in a Japanese jour-nal of Sōen Nakagawa, then a Zen monk in seclusion at Mt. Dai-bosatsu in Yamanashi Prefecture of Japan. Senzaki was im-pressed by the story of a monk who left "Cathedral Zen" behind and sought his own realization in a little hut in the mountains. He wrote to him, and the two monks corresponded for several years. It was arranged that Nakagawa would visit Los Angeles, but the war interfered with these plans, and delayed them until 1949.

Meanwhile, Senzaki, Mrs. Tanahashi, and others in the Jap-anese community of Los Angeles were interned at Heart Moun-tain Relocation Camp in Wyoming. This was disruptive and de-moralizing for everyone, but the people who had by now gathered about Senzaki made the best of their situation. They practiced zazen together, recited sutras, and studied the Dharma. Senzaki's American students were also supportive. Ruth Strout McCand-less kept his library, each Japanese volume numbered, and when he needed a book, he would request it by number, and she would mail it to him.

After the war Senzaki returned to Los Angeles, and was given a room rent-free on the top floor of the Miyako Hotel by the owner, a fellow internee. It was here that I met him in December 1947. At this time he had perhaps thirty American students and another thirty followers who had been with him at Heart Moun-tain. Fifteen to eighteen English-speaking students would crowd into his room for zazen and a lecture two evenings a week. The Japanese students would come for sutras and zazen on Sunday mornings. We sat on folding chairs, and there was very little ceremony.

We had, moreover, no membership arrangement, and no organizational structure. Ironically, this anarchistic arrangement meant that our teacher made all the decisions in a benevolent, but authoritarian manner. We were content with this process. He was our wise, gentle teacher, and we could only be followers.

A tolerant teacher as well: Senzaki was not only infinitely patient with us, he welcomed visitors warmly, even Theosophists and spiritualists whose ideas he found ridiculous. I remember one day overhearing his conversation with someone who was holding forth on the occult mysteries of the Pyramids, and his part in the discussion was to say respectfully at intervals, "Oh, really? I didn't know that."

He was especially tolerant of other forms of Buddhism. "Buddhism is a single stream," he would say, and he deliberately used classical terms in their Pali pronunciations, in keeping with Theravada tradition, rather than in the Sanskrit of the Mahayana. For example, he always said (and wrote) "Dhamma" rather than "Dharma." He was friendly with the only Theravada Buddhist teacher in Los Angeles at that time, and often invited him to speak to us.

I have never known a teacher more down to earth in his terminology. Once when I was cleaning the dōjō, he was in the library speaking with visitors about his heritage. At one point he raised his voice and said to me, "Please bring me the picture of that old fellow on the table." The old fellow was Bodhidharma, and the table was his altar. Of course Bodhidharma was his inspiration and the table was the devotional center of his practice, but for him these were matters that were better understated.

Senzaki was a calm and jovial man, at home in the New World, who loved to visit the Sweet Shop in Japan Town with a few friends for a waffle. He walked rapidly, always leading the way, posture very erect for his rather stout figure, with a ready smile and a greeting for his many friends. His clothing was tweedy and rumpled, and for Zen meetings he would simply wear a robe over his street clothes.

In the meetings his talks were full of Zen stories, incomprehensible, but delightful. We lived in hopes that we would gradually come to understand them, assured by his words, "Zen is not a puzzle; it cannot be solved by wit. It is spiritual food for those who want to learn what life is and what our mission is."[6] He included personal interviews in the schedule of meetings in early years, but discontinued this practice before I began attending.

Senzaki felt he was just introducing Zen practice to the United States. "Someday the Mentorgarten will disappear," he said to me, "but Sōen San will build a great temple in the United States and the Dhamma will flourish." Sōen San, however, became Sōen Rōshi and abbot of a monastery in Japan, and the best he could do was visit.

Like Hotei, however, Senzaki has many descendents. His friend Sōen Rōshi encouraged Mentorgarten students to persevere, and in turn influenced his friend Rōshi Haku'un Yasutani to visit the United States and lead retreats during the 1960s. Thus the two rōshis continued Senzaki's work and in time inspired the development of a number of American centers. The Diamond Sangha in Hawaii, the Zen Center of Los Angeles, the Zen Studies Society in New York, and the Rochester Zen Center—all can trace their heritage through the gentle train of karma that Senzaki began. Members of the San Francisco Zen Center and of other groups, as well as many individual Zen students, feel an affinity with him.

Senzaki lived out his last years in a flat rented for him by Mrs. Tanahashi in Boyle Heights in east Los Angeles, after the Miyako Hotel was sold. He continued to meet with students almost to the

[6]Nyogen Senzaki, "Realization." In *Namu Dai Bosa*, edited by Louis Nordstrom.

end, and taped his last words before he died in March 1958. I vividly remember sitting in the funeral parlor and listening to him speak for the last time:

> Friends in Dhamma, be satisfied with your own head. Do not put any false heads above your own. Then minute after minute, watch your steps closely. Always keep your head cold and your feet warm. These are my last words to you

Then he added, "Thank you very much, everybody, for taking such good care of me for so long. Bye bye." And the tape ended with his little laugh.

I am pleased that *Buddhism and Zen*, the collection of his essays that he assembled in collaboration with Ruth Strout McCandless, is now being reissued. I feel his presence as I read his words:

> America has had Zen students in the past, has them in the present, and will have many of them in the future. They mingle easily with so-called worldlings. They play with children; respect kings and beggars, and handle gold and silver as pebbles and stones.

These are words of prophecy, and they are also vows. I make them my own.

Robert Aitken
Koko An Zendo, Honolulu
Spring Training Period, 1987

The Buddha-body is omnipresent.
Each sentient being beholds it
Through aspiration and Karma relation
As it dwells eternally on this seat of meditation. *

*It is the inherent nature of the Buddha-body that it individualizes itself in myriad manifestations in the phenomenal world. It does not stand alone outside particular existences but abides in them, animates them, and makes them move freely. In this form, it is subjected to certain conditions such as time, space, and causation. Its essence is infinite, but its manifestations are finite and limited. It is for this reason that the Buddha-body has to wait until conditions are matured before expressing itself.

Suppose that there is a mirror. . . the mirror of the Buddha-body. Anything that comes in front of it is reflected without any premeditation on the part of the mirror. Beautiful or ugly, high or low, rich or poor, good or evil, everything is reflected impartially. Wherever and whenever conditions are correct, all particular things will be reflected in the mirror or Mind-Essence of the Buddha-body without hesitation, without reasoning, without demonstration. It is thus that the principle of karma works.

Although things are many and subject to constant transformation and regulation by their karma, the Buddha-body abides eternally on the seat of Bodhi, our inmost being.

The moon is shining serenely in the sky, casting her reflection in countless places wherever conditions are matured. We see her image on the smallest trace of water or on a vast expanse, which may be polluted or clean, but each reflects the same moon according to its nature. The shadows also are as numerous as the bodies of water, but we cannot say that one shadow is essentially different from another, nor that the moon left her orbit even for a moment.

BUDDHISM
and ZEN

Ten Questions

Buddhism is no longer considered a strange teaching filled with superstition and idol worship, but is now understood by the intellectual people of the world as a religion of enlightenment entirely in accord with the latest findings of science and the highest of ethics. With the increase of Western interest in Buddhism has come the desire for precise and uncolored information. Philologists may translate the scriptures and commentaries faithfully, but without a deeper understanding of their meaning, the words can be misleading or insignificant. Priests from the temples are often anxious to increase the membership of their congregations, so we find them stressing outward conformity at the price of inner development. It is an accepted fact that all major religions have been altered and many of their concepts distorted by those whose lives were allegedly dedicated to the continuation and dissemination of their teachings. Also, religions are typically affected by the earlier beliefs and practices indigenous to varying peoples.

Buddhism is divided into two groups often referred to as Hinayana and Mahayana. In general, the difference is that one may be described as retiring from the world to seek enlightenment for oneself and the other as remaining in the world to enlighten oneself and others. Although there are sects within each of these groups, all are united in the basic teachings as given by Gautama Buddha.

The following ten questions are those most frequently asked by non-Buddhists:

What does a Buddhist believe or worship?
The words "believe" and "worship" are unfamiliar to Buddhists because they do not "believe" but understand, and they do not "worship" but practice what they understand.

Is Buddha an Oriental god?
The answer is *no*. Buddha was a human being, a student of philosophy and a seeker of ultimate truth. He was born Gautama Siddhartha, crown prince of Nepal, 565 years before the Christian era. When he was twenty-nine years old, he renounced his position to become a mendicant monk, and after six years of hard work, he became enlightened through his meditation. He then traveled and taught among the people of India for forty-five years. His teachings were recorded in Sanskrit and Pali, and later translated into Chinese, Japanese, and other Asiatic languages. At the present time, only about nine percent of these scriptures have been translated into Western languages. English philologists and archeologists did much of the early work of translating, then the Germans, French, and Scandinavians followed with books in their own tongues. American students, who are more interested in the spirit of Buddhism and the practical application of the teachings, now have two main currents of Buddhist thought from which to draw, the Oriental and Occidental.

On his deathbed Buddha said, "The teachings I have given you will be your teacher when I am gone." He called the whole system of his teachings, *Dharma* or *Dhamma*, the law of the universe. Buddhism is a teaching that will free our minds to come into harmony with this universal law. As such, this teaching is gradually becoming the invisible treasure of intellectual people the world over.

If Buddha is not a god, then there must be a real god above us. Do Buddhists believe in a god?
If the word "God" refers to a poetical expression of universal law, then the answer is yes. But if the term refers to a personal existence apart from universal law, then the answer is no. Buddhists un-

derstand the universe and God as one. There is no remainder in the mathematics of infinity. All life is one; therefore, there cannot be God and man, nor a universe and God. A god not in the world is a false god, and a world not in God is unreal. All things return to one, and one operates in all.

A person is not unmoral or a heathen for not believing in a personal god. On the contrary, such a person may know the true nature of humankind and the universe better than more orthodox followers of younger religions. Buddhists, for example, left anthropomorphic ideas behind twenty-five centuries ago.

If there is no god outside this world, who created the world?
If you are so attached to the word "God," then the universe is God and God is the universe. To say that God created the universe, and then to say that he stands outside this universe is a contradiction. Neither God nor non-God can exist outside this oneness. We create the world anew each moment of each day. When we are asleep, there is nothing, but once we are awake, then the world of form, color, odor, taste, and touch are instantly created by our senses. Buddhists see the world as a phenomenon of flux consisting of various relations, but not created by a divinity.

This world is conceived in the relationship between subjectivity and objectivity. Buddha concluded that without this relationship of the world to the elements, subjective and objective, there is nothing. If you believe this world is created by a supreme being, then you must feel powerless to change it, thus leaving your fate to the mercy of the creator. Buddhists know that the world is your own production. You may change it, rebuild it, or improve it to suit your own will.

Then what is the mind? Was not this mind given by God at the very beginning?
If there is no personal God, then no one but you can create the mind. The mind is an endless chain of three processes, namely, craving, acting, and discontent. These three represent a cycle:

craving to acting, acting to discontent, and discontent to craving. Without these three processes there is no mind and, consequently, no body. When this level of understanding is achieved,
it will be seen that everything in the universe operates according
to these processes, under the law of causation, and aside from this
endless chain there is no creator and no ruler of the universe.
Buddhism places the center of the universe in the subjectivity of
the individual mind, whereas other religions place it in the objectivity outside of the mind.

What is the first cause, the very beginning of everything?
Some religions answer God, Allah, Brahma, or something else
outside of the individual. Buddhism sweeps aside idle speculation and teaches you to find the answer in your own realization.
Your intellection will not solve the problem, but will use time to
push the solution farther from you. Buddhism does not ask you
to believe that you yourself are the creator, nor to accept the prop-
osition that you are not making vicarious atonement for the
transgressions of another, but it does promise that when you have
fulfilled the requirements, you will know the answer.

Do Buddhists believe in a future life?
Yes, if a future life refers to the continuation of cosmic life, but
no, if it refers to a later individual life. We are living in an endless
world, the world of karmic life or the world of three processes.
Other religions teach that your life comes to an end and you receive judgment, but Buddhism teaches that good or bad characters continue according to individual desire. In other religions,
past, present, and future are set in a straight line, but to Buddhists
they are mere names for an endless cycle.

*Does the word Buddha ever signify anything other than the man
who proclaimed these teachings?*
Yes. The word "Buddha" suggests an enlightened mental state or

condition. Oftentimes the term means this alone. Gautama Siddhartha was called Buddha because he attained supreme knowledge and moral perfection through his own perseverance, but he was neither a god revealing himself to mankind nor one sent by a god to bring salvation to the world. He attained his realization through his own striving without seeking help from a god or man. Although Buddhists refer to Gautama Siddhartha as Buddha, they also recognize other Buddhas both before and since his time. Buddhahood is the goal that anyone can attain. But there is no saving power to it. Buddhists believe there is no savior outside the brilliancy of enlightened wisdom.

If you have a figure or picture of Buddha in your home, do not worship it or pray to it for fortune or health. Keep it as a reminder of your own future being. As you learn meditation, the calm poise depicted will be your good companion. Bear in mind Buddha's words, "If you try to see me through my form, or if you try to hear me through my voice, you will never reach me and will remain forever a stranger to my teaching."

Are there precepts in Buddhism comparable to the Ten
Commandments or the Sermon on the Mount?
Yes. Buddhist monks and nuns keep more than two hundred and fifty precepts. The *Brahmajala Sutra* lists ten precepts for all Mahayana Buddhists to keep. American Buddhists keep three precepts: to avoid all evil thoughts and evil actions; to attain good thoughts and right actions; and to develop *Prajna*[1] so that all humanity is benefited and all sentient beings mercifully treated.

From these precepts it follows naturally that no living thing is killed for individual pleasure—there is loving-kindness for all sentient beings; nothing is taken which does not belong to one—live an unselfish and generous life; in marriage keep constancy strictly with love and respect for each other—purify and refine

[1] Prajna (Sanskrit): wisdom; that ability to see directly into the true nature of things beyond mere intellection.

yourself; speak no word that is not true—develop integrity in every way; avoid intoxication and lead a pure and sober life: keep yourself clean and worthy.

What is the attitude of Buddhism toward other religions?
"Buddhism has no destructive intention against other religions. This is the distinctive mark by which Buddhist missionary work is differentiated from the work of Christian and Moslem missionaries. The Christian-Moslem view has usually been that destruction must precede construction, or at any rate, that the two must go hand in hand. The Buddhist aim has been, usually, to do no destroying and to put all its emphasis on the constructive and positive side."[2] There is no bloodstain on the history of Buddhist proselytizers; in no instance have they tried to destroy the customs of other faiths or countries by ridicule or force, neither do they insist on the exclusive use of their own rituals or rites. They accept what is true and beautiful in every religion, and they study the scriptures and teachings of all faiths. Buddhism is spread by the quiet influence of those who live its teachings day by day, and through the information given in universities, colleges, and libraries throughout the world.

[2] James Bissett Pratt, Ph.D., *The Pilgrimage of Buddhism* (New York: Macmillan Co., 1928).

Notes on Meditation

Although the word "Zen" is derived from the Chinese translit-
eration of the Sanskrit dhyana,[1] it is not the same as dhyana.
Daito once said, "One may pass hours sitting in contemplation,
but if he has no Zen, he is not my disciple." On another occa-
sion a student came to Kwan-Zan to receive personal guidance.
Kwan-Zan asked him where he had studied Zen and under which
master. When the student replied that he had studied under Jaku-
shitsu of Yoken Monastery, Kwan-Zan said, "Show me what you
have learned." The student's answer was to sit cross-legged in silence, whereupon Kwan-Zan shouted, "My monastery has too
many stone Buddhas. We need no more. Get out, you good-for-
nothing!"

Zen uses meditation as a means of entering *Samadhi*,[2] but it
does not deny the existence of other methods; however, it does
insist that what is gained by the practice of Zazen[3] must be applied
practically in everyday life. The teachings of Zen warn constantly of falling into the trap of "quietism."

When one devotes oneself to meditation, mental burdens, unnecessary worries, and wandering thoughts drop off one by one;
life seems to run smoothly and pleasantly. A student may now
depend on intuition to make decisions. As one acts on intuition,

[1] Dhyana (Sanskrit): meditation.
[2] Samadhi (Sanskrit): is sometimes used in place of dhyana, but more often is referred to as that condition achieved by the practice of dhyana.
[3] Zazen (from Chinese *tso ch'an*): to sit in meditation.

second thought, with its dualism, doubt, and hesitation, does not arise.

Consciousness is not an entity ruling the movements of the mind, but a focus of mental powers. When mental activities cease working in meditation, there is no focus. But the moment the five senses begin to work, the consciousness is alerted. It is precisely the same as when a person awakes from sleep.

Sometimes beginners in meditation speak about their dreams as though there was some connection between Zen realization and dreaming. Dreams, however, are a psychological phenomenon and have nothing to do with Zen.

Koan

A koan is a problem given by a teacher to a student for solution. The student must solve it primarily alone, although a teacher will occasionally give some help. To work upon a koan, you must be eager to solve it; to solve a koan, you must face it without thinking of it. The more you pound it in cognition, the more difficult it will be to obtain a solution. Two hands brought together produce a sound. What is the sound of one hand? This is a koan. If you think that there is no such sound, you are mistaken.

A Zen koan is nothing but nonsense to outsiders, but for a student of Zen it is a gate to enlightenment. Intellectual gymnastics, no matter how superior or refined, could never solve a koan; in fact, a koan is given to force a student beyond intellection. Do not work upon more than one koan at a time, and do not discuss a koan with any person other than your teacher. Just face the question without thinking about anything else. Without neglecting everyday duties your every leisure moment should be spent exercising the mind with the koan.

Each koan is an expression of a person's actual experience, directly from personal attainment. When you reach the same stage, you will express the same thing. Unless you attain realization for yourself, it is useless for philosophers or spiritual teachers to talk about noumenon, oneness, the absolute, God within you or any other empty name, which will only serve to lead you astray.

Unless you have faith in being enlightened in this life, you had better not study Zen at all. There are plenty of sects promising enlightenment *after* death.

Before you enter one of the gates of Zen, you must strip yourself of egoistic ideas. If you think you can reason out the final truth with your brain, why do you not do it? Once you begin your work in Zen, do not turn to the left nor to the right but keep going straight ahead.

Ekido, a Zen master of Japan, who lived in the nineteenth century, made the following vows: first, the cascade of life and death must be crossed over. (What is life? What is death? These questions must be answered.) Until the dawn of such realization, I will not stop my meditation. Second, every hour of the day and night must be lived as the Buddhas and patriarchs lived. Their way is untransmissible and can be attained only by living. Third, wherever I am, whenever I live, I should not have any secondary thought for environment, favorable or adverse.

The average man does not know the true meaning of life and death, so he clings to life and is afraid of death. A Bodhisattva does not hold his body as his own, nor does he see mind and body as being separate. When he recognizes it by the senses, he calls it body, when he sees it by introspection, he names it mind. Most people cling to "their" thoughts, thus causing suffering in the world. In the *Diamond Sutra*, Buddha said, "In case good men and women raise the desire for supreme enlightenment, they should thus keep their thoughts under control. If a Bodhisattva[4] retains the thought of an ego, a person, a being, or a soul, he is no more a Bodhisattva." My logic can convince your reason, but I cannot overcome the inertia of your dualistic thinking. Your

[4]Bodhisattva: a person dedicated not only to his own enlightenment but also to the enlightenment of all sentient beings, and in this way distinct from *Ahrat*.

intellect may comprehend the oneness of all things, but your thinking, like a cascade, will continue to flow dually. You must cross this cascade once and for all to see for yourself the true emptiness of which Buddha said, "All that has form is an illusive existence. When it is perceived that all form is no-form, the *Tathagata*[5] is recognized."

"Every hour in the day and every hour in the night I will try to live as Buddhas and patriarchs lived." Buddhism does not seek adherents. If you desire worldly fame in any form, then work for that instead of hiding yourself under the name of "Buddhist." "Their way is untransmissible. . . ." Live the life and you will know. When Zen says, "Dharma was transmitted from a teacher to a disciple," it means only that the disciple perceived enlightenment for himself, thereby "receiving the Lamp of Dharma."

"I should not have any secondary thought for environment." Do not try to cling to pleasures. It is as impossible as attempting to capture sunshine in a box. Do not stop your tears. It will not help you to ask why you are sad. Avoid secondary thought. All things are transient, your happiness as well as your sorrow, and secondary thoughts will bring you nothing but suffering.

> The bamboo shadows are sweeping the stairs,
> But no dust is stirred.
> The moonlight penetrates the depths of the pool,
> But no trace is left in the water.

Emptiness

Emptiness is a term used in Buddhism that has caused considerable misunderstanding in Western minds. When a Buddhist speaks of emptiness, he does not intend it to signify the opposite of fullness, but rather that unconditioned state in which there is nothing to be given and nothing to be received. Since it cannot be expressed in speech, it can only be hinted at in dialogue or referred to by use of the word "emptiness."

[5]Tathagata: Buddha; Mind Essence; Eternal Presence; Eternal Now.

Some students have advanced far enough in their meditation to empty their minds, but once they resume their normal activity, they are as unstable as before. In effect, they continue a condition of mind in which they recognize that there is nothing, not realizing that this in itself is a concrete, self-limiting state quite different from the "emptiness" of Buddhism.

True emptiness cannot be included nor excluded. When you count your inhalations and exhalations, contending thoughts will gradually disappear, leaving no trace. Meditation? Emptiness? Realization? Buddha? Leave them all behind. Your everyday life will become calm and peaceful, making you less worried and less anxious. At a glance you will recognize your real self.

Karma

Karma is a Sanskrit noun in the nominative case derived from the verb *Kar*, meaning *to do*; in the objective case it is *Karman*. *Kamma* and *Kamman* are the Pali equivalents. All states and conditions in this life are the direct results of previous actions, and each action in the present determines the fate of the future. Life is the working process of *Karman*, the endless series of cause and effect.

In the *Dhammapada*, Buddha said: "All that is, is the result of thought, it is founded on thought, it is made of thought. If a man speaks or acts with an evil thought, pain follows him, as the wheel follows the foot of the ox that draws the carriage. All that is, is the result of thought, it is founded on thought, it is made of thought. If a man speaks or acts with a pure thought, happiness follows him, like a shadow that never leaves him."

Buddhism teaches the way to emancipation and enlightenment, but Gautama Buddha never suggested that the way to perfection was easy or simple. Before he achieved his own enlightenment, he experienced tremendous difficulties. The natural tendency of every man is toward ease, comfort, and the "good" things of life, but if he wants to climb the upward path, he must toil hard. His aspiration for perfection must be accomplished by self-discipline. Deliverance is not to be attained by prayer, belief in creeds, nor initiation into secret orders or mysteries, but by leading an upright, worthy life. Purification is accomplished by being conscious of every thought, word, and act, and by the avoidance of evil out of respect to life. To respect life is to practice the ordinary virtues, to be honest, to live cleanly and to think purely, to be just and kind, to respect others and to live in peace with them, and to strive against ignorance.

Buddha is a state of mind, an intellectual and moral perfection. It means enlightenment: One who is truly enlightened is a Buddha. Buddha Sakyamuni attained Buddhahood through his own efforts and declared that it was possible for anyone to do the same. By your own efforts you must find the inner treasure and see it for yourself.

Bodhi-Dharma once said, "If you wish to see the Buddha, you must look into your own inner-nature; this nature is the Buddha himself. If you have not seen your own nature, what is the use of thinking of Buddha, or reciting Sutras, or fasting, or keeping the precepts? By thinking of Buddha, your meritorious deed will bear fruit; by reciting the Sutras, you may attain a bright intellect; by keeping the precepts, you may be born into the heavens; by practicing charity, you may be rewarded abundantly; but as to seeking the Buddha, you are far away."

Dōgen's Practice of Meditation

Truth is perfect and complete in itself. It is not something newly discovered; it has always existed.

Truth is not far away; it is ever near.

Do not follow some other person's thoughts, but learn to listen to the voice within yourself. Your body and your mind will blend in unity, and you will realize the oneness of all life.

Even a delicate movement of your dualistic thought will prevent you from entering *Samadhi*, the Palace of Meditation. (The

Sanskrit *samadhi* is sometimes used in place of *dhyana*, but more often refers to the condition achieved by the practice of dhyana.)

Those who talk much about realization are usually wandering outside its gates, and will have some struggle before they enter this Palace of Meditation.

Buddha Sakyamuni meditated for six years, and Bodhi-Dharma meditated for nine years. The practice of meditation is not a method for the attainment of realization but is enlightenment itself.

Your search among books, word upon word, may lead you to the depths of the cognitive world, but it is not the way to receive the reflection of your true self.

When you have thrown off your ideas as to mind and body, you will see the original person in full. Zen is nothing but the actualization of truth; therefore, the longings that are followed by actions are not the true attitude of Zen at all.

To attain the blessedness of meditation you should begin the practice with a pure motive and a firm determination. Your room for meditation must be clean and quiet. Take your regular meal sparingly, and shut out all noises and disturbances. Do not let the mind dwell in thought on what is good or what is bad. Just relax and forget that you are meditating. Do not desire to become a Buddha. If you do, you will never become one.

Sit down in a chair with a large cushion in a manner as comfortable as possible. Wear loose clothing and remove your shoes, but keep your feet warm.

Put your right hand on your left thigh, palm up, and let it hold the four fingers of your left hand so that the left thumb may press down the right thumb. Hold your body straight. Lean not to the left nor to the right. Do not tip forward nor bend to the back. Your ears should be at right angles to your shoulders, and your nose on a straight line with your navel. Keep your tongue at the roof of your mouth and close your lips and teeth firmly. Keep your eyes slightly open, and breathe through your nostrils.

Before you begin meditation, move your body from right to left a few times, then take several slow, deep breaths. Hold your body erect, allowing your breathing to become normal again. Many thoughts will crowd into your mind . . . ignore them until they vanish. Do not allow the mind to become negative. Think that which you cannot think. In other words, think nothing. This is the proper way to meditate according to Zen teaching.

Zen meditation is not physical culture, nor is it a method to gain something material. It is peacefulness and blessedness itself. It is the actualization of the Buddha-Dharma,[6] namely, the ultimate truth of universal oneness.

In your meditation you yourself are the mirror reflecting the solution of your problems. The human mind has absolute freedom within its true nature. You can attain your emancipation intuitively. Do not work for emancipation. Instead, allow the work itself to be your emancipation.

When you wish to stop, stand up slowly. Practice this meditation in the morning, in the evening, or at any leisure time. You will soon realize that your mental burdens are dropping away from you one by one, and that you are gaining a sort of intuitive power hitherto unnoticed. Do not think that the wise do not need to meditate. The wise and the dull should both take time for meditation. Constant practice will lead anyone to the realization of truth.

In Oriental countries there have been many thousands of students who have practiced Zen meditation and obtained its fruits. Do not doubt its possibilities because of the simplicity of its method. If you cannot find the truth within yourself, where else do you expect to find it?

Life is short and no one knows what the next moment will bring. Cultivate your mind while you have the opportunity, thereby gaining the treasures of wisdom, which in turn you can share abundantly with others, bringing them happiness.

—Dōgen (1200–1253 A.D.)

[6]Buddha-Dharma (Sanskrit; Buddha-Dhamma in Pali): enlightened wisdom.

Each one of us should try to be the master of his own mind and body, to govern his environment peacefully, to lead a pure and unselfish life, and to be kind and helpful to all fellow beings. These are our most important daily tasks.

Zen Buddhism is the vehicle of *Buddha-hrydaya*, the brilliancy of enlightenment, the highest and most essential of all teaching. This enlightenment is not confined to hermitages in remote mountains; it transcends all customs, all sects, all life, all places, and all time, and is as applicable in a busy city as in a quiet suburb.

As to the place where you meditate, as well as the conditions for its practice and continuance, there are ten essential requirements (although these rules for meditation apply in general to all who practice Zen meditation, they are especially important for beginners; later meditation can be done under conditions not suitable for beginners):

1. The place should be clean and quiet.
2. Its temperature should be comfortable during all seasons.
3. It should be well ventilated.
4. The weather should be neither too warm nor too cold.
5. The place should be neither too dark nor too light.
6. It should not offer any view that might be distracting.
7. Beginners in meditation should avoid association with either well-known or argumentative people.
8. Beginners should avoid those who are competitive.
9. Beginners should avoid all places and situations such as fire, flood, and the haunts of criminals.
10. Beginners should not meditate by the sea or in the vicinity of popular resorts.

Regarding your physical condition:

1. Be sure your stomach is neither empty nor full.
2. Dress comfortably in clean clothes.
3. Regulate your hours of sleep.
4. Set aside leisure hours for meditation.

5. Do not spend time writing poems or essays on Zen.
6. Do not meditate immediately after meals.
7. Do not meditate when you are nervous.
8. Remove your shoes while meditating.
9. Bathe daily.
10. Since a healthy body means healthy meditation, take care of your health.

There are also ten things you should know about your mind as you learn meditation:

1. Do not think of either good or bad nor of right and wrong.
2. Do not think of either the past or the future. The present moment should contain your entire universe during meditation.
3. Do not be overly ambitious to attain realization. Do not desire to become a Buddha.
4. Both before and after meditation think of *Anicca*, impermanency; think also of *Anatta*, the impossibility of identifying any self-entity in either your mind or your body.
5. Do not cling to subjectivity; do not cling to objectivity. Non-thinking and non-clinging purify the mind.
6. Before and after meditation repeat your vow to save all sentient beings.[7]
7. When your mind wanders, clasp your hands tightly, or concentrate upon the tip of your nose. Usually awareness of the lower part of your abdomen prevents mind-wandering.
8. If you feel dizzy during meditation, concentrate your mind upon your forehead.

[7]The Bodhisattva's Vow:
However innumerable sentient beings may be, I vow to save them all;
However inexhaustible the evil passions are, I vow to destroy them;
However immeasurable the sacred teachings are, I vow to learn them all;
No matter how difficult the path of Buddhahood may be,
I vow to follow it to the end.

9. If you feel sick, concentrate your mind upon your toes. (Zen students should always remain aware of their feet when walking.)

10. Without moving or holding anything in your mind, or clinging either to a positive or negative idea, advance step-by-step ahead in your meditation until you hear the sound of one hand.

—Some items translated from Keizan (1268–1325 A.D.)

When speaking to his disciples about meditation, Joshu, an old master, once said, "If you follow my instruction and do not attain enlightenment, you may cut off my head."

When you meditate, you must have nothing in front and nothing in back. Erase your memories of the past; cancel your hopes for the future. In that moment there is neither time nor space . . . there is only the eternal present. Zen calls this condition of the mind the "moment of great death." Do not be afraid of this stage in your meditation. Instead of forcing yourself to enter such a condition, just meditate faithfully, either by counting your breath or meditating on your koan and you will arrive there naturally and gracefully without even being aware of it. This is the "gateless gate" of Zen. Until you pass this gate, you cannot enter Zen, but once you have passed it, you will realize that it never existed.

A monk once went to a teacher for personal guidance. The teacher said, "When I clap my hands together, there is a sound. What is the sound of one hand?" Although the monk worked hard, he could not solve this koan. "You are not working hard enough," his teacher told him. "You are attached to food, sleep, name, and fame." The next time the monk appeared before his teacher, he fell over as though dead. "You are dead, all right," observed the teacher, "but what about the sound of one hand?" The monk looked up from where he lay on the floor. "I have not solved that as yet." "A dead man tells no story," said the teacher. "Get out, you rascal!" This monk had his teacher in mind all the time.

Instead of striving for something to be added to your nature, get rid of all unnecessary opinion, prejudice, pride, and the hundred other things that restrict you. Even your desire for enlightenment will be an obstacle. Just go quietly ahead in your meditation step-by-step without thought of good or bad, success or failure. "Do not linger where the Buddha is, and where the Buddha is not, pass on quickly."

Nanin, a master during the Meiji era, received a university professor who came to inquire about Zen.

Nanin served tea. He poured his visitor's cup full, and then kept on pouring.

The professor watched the overflow until he could no longer restrain himself. "It is overfull. No more will go in!"

"Like this cup," Nanin replied, "you are full of your own opinions and speculations. How can I show you Zen unless you first empty your cup?"[8]

[8] Nyogen Senzaki and Paul Reps, 101 Zen Stories.

Shodoka

Yokadaishi (Yung Chia) was an outstanding disciple of Yeno (Hui-neng), the Sixth Patriarch. Shodoka (Song of Realization) is one of a number of works on the Zen approach to enlightenment left by Yokadaishi when he died in 713 A.D. The story of Yoka is contained in the *Dankyō*, a writing of the Sixth Patriarch:

Zen Master Genkaku of Yoka was born of a Tai family in the state of Onshu. As a youth he studied the Sutras and *Shastras*,[1] and was well versed in the teaching of *Samatha*[2] and *Vipassana*.[3] Through the reading of the *Vimalakirti Nirdesa Sutra*,[4] he realized intuitively the mystery of his own mind, that is, he realized Mind-Essence.

A disciple of the Sixth Patriarch by the name of Gensaku paid him a visit, and during the course of the discussion, noticed that the comments of his friend agreed with the sayings of the various patriarchs. He then asked, "May I know the name of your teacher who transmitted the Dharma to you?"

"I had teachers to instruct me," replied Genkaku, "when I studied the Sutras and *Shastras* of the *Vaipulya* section, but it was through the reading of the *Vimalakirti Nirdesa Sutra* that I realized the significance of the *Buddacitta* (Buddha-heart)

[1] Shastras or Sastras: commentaries on the Sutras.
[2] Samatha: quietude.
[3] Vipassana: contemplation or discernment (Tendai School).
[4] Vimalakirti Nirdesa Sutra (Sanskrit): A book of Buddha's teachings.

Dhyana School and in this respect I have not yet had a teacher to verify and confirm my attainment."

"Before the time of the remote Buddhas," Gensaku remarked, "it was possible to dispense with the service of a teacher, but since that time, he who attains enlightenment without the aid and confirmation of a teacher is a natural heretic."

"Will you kindly act as my testifier?" asked Genkaku.

"My words carry no weight," replied his friend. "In Sokei the Sixth Patriarch is to be found to whom visitors in great numbers come from all directions with the common object of having the Dharma transmitted to them. If you wish to go there, I shall be glad to accompany you."

When they reached Sokei to interview the patriarch, Genkaku walked around him three times, then stood still without making obeisance to him.

Noting his discourtesy, the patriarch said, "A Buddhist monk is the embodiment of three thousand moral precepts and eighty thousand minor disciplinary rules. . . . I wonder where you come from and what makes you so conceited."

"Since the question of incessant rebirth is a momentous one and death may come at any moment, I have no time to waste on ceremony, and wish you to give me a quick answer to this problem."

"Why do you not realize the principle of 'Birthlessness' and thus solve the problem of the transiency of life?" the patriarch retorted.

"To realize the essence of mind is to be free of rebirth," Genkaku replied, "and once this problem is solved, the question of transiency exists no longer."

"That is so. That is so," the patriarch concurred.

At this moment Genkaku made obeisance according to the ceremony of departure.

"You are going away too quickly, are you not?" asked the patriarch.

"How can there be 'quickness' when motion does not exist intrinsically?" Genkaku answered.

"Who knows that motion does not exist?" asked the patriarch.

"I hope you will not particularize," Genkaku observed.

The patriarch then commended him for his thorough grasp of the idea of "Birthlessness," but Genkaku countered, "Is there an idea in 'Birthlessness'?"

"Without an idea, who can particularize?" asked the patriarch.

"That which particularizes is not an idea," replied Genkaku.

"Well said!" exclaimed the patriarch. He then asked Genkaku to delay his departure and spend the night there. From that time on Genkaku was known to his contemporaries as the "Enlightened-One-Who-Had-Spent-a-Night-With-The-Patriarch."

Shodoka is memorized in its entirety by students in China, Korea, and Japan, and they are often inspired during its recitation.

In the *Shodoka* that follows the stanzas come directly from a copy of the original, in a free translation by Nyogen Senzaki. The commentary, separated from each stanza, is Nyogen Senzaki's own instruction to his students, and is intended to assist the reader in his understanding and interpretation of the poem.

Shodoka

BY YOKADAISHI

Do you see that Zen student? He has forgotten what he has
learned, yet he practices easily and freely what he has learned
and also what he should learn.

He lives in equanimity calmly and contentedly. He is free of all
care, yet he acts naturally and reasonably.

He neither strives to avoid delusion nor searches after truth. He
knows delusions as baseless and truth as himself.

He sees the true nature of ignorance as Buddha-nature, and the
true body of his illusionary body as *Dharma-kaya*,[1] the Buddha's eternal body.

Yokadaishi is admiring and praising the Zen student. He sees a
person who has gone beyond relative good and evil, and who
leaves no trace of his learning nor shadow of his doing. He is a
sage who does not look like a sage, and he is a philosopher who
does not carry the odor of philosophy.

If you try to avoid idle thoughts or delusions when you meditate, you cannot enter *Samadhi*. Whoever seeks after the truth
will remain behind the truth. What you consider idle thoughts
or delusions are nothing but waves on the vast ocean of Buddha-
nature. Just as there are no waves apart from the water, there is
no delusion, no idle thought, no ignorance separate from Buddha-nature.

[1] Dharma-kaya (Sanskrit): Law body of the Buddha.

Since our bodies are impermanent, it follows that they are also empty and visionary. In fact, they do not even really belong to us. Your body is not yours, and my body is not mine.

> When one realizes completely the *Dharma-body*,[2] one sees no object.
> He, himself, is the source of all things, and his true nature is another name of the eternal Buddha.
> Material things and mental phenomena come and go like clouds in the blue sky.
> Greed, anger, and ignorance . . . these three foams appear and disappear like a mirage on the ocean.

When one recognizes the Dharma-body as such, no matter how beautifully he may define it or describe it, he is still lingering in dualism. But once he has unified himself with the Dharma-body, there is no more and there is no less. He is the Dharma-body, and the Dharma-body is he. He is the source of all things in the universe. His true nature is the eternal Buddha that was never born and will never die.

Greed, anger, and ignorance are the three poisons injurious to the good character of man.

A Tibetan Buddhist once wrote: "Greed, anger, and ignorance . . . these three stand as obstacles to the way of deliverance; they prevent us in the growth of insight as the roots of the couch-grass prevent the growth of useful plants. If there exist in countries other than Tibet people who have experienced the truth, I cannot say. But I know that among the mighty mountains of my native land there are men and women who can bear witness that in this very life they have attained the supreme goal and tasted the ultimate deliverance. One must not expect that these enlightened ones will come to live with worldlings, whose most serious actions appear as the play of small children."

This mountaineer does not know Zen at all! Zen students never run away from the three poisons, but see them only as an

[2]Dharma-body: original person in full; the sound of one hand; the eternal Buddha.

ephemeral mirage. America has had Zen students in the past, has them in the present, and will have many of them in the future. They mingle easily with so-called worldlings. They play with children, respect kings and beggars, and handle gold and silver as pebbles and stones.

> When he realizes the truth, he has no delusion concerning his personal desires nor his self-limited ideas.
> He knows that there is no ego entity existing in him, and sees clearly the voidness of all form as merely shadow in relation to both subjective and objective elements.
> If you live in this Zen, you can leave hell in your dreams of yesterday, and make your own paradise wherever you stand.
> Those without realization, who cheat people with false knowledge, will create a hell during their own lives.

Zen aims at nothing but realization or attainment. Philosophers may postulate reality, driving themselves to the end of the trail of logic, but none of them ever succeeds in attaining. To follow logic and believe that something *must be* is one thing, but to experience it is another. When Zen asks to hear the sound of one hand, it demands actual experience and nothing else. A student may say that this is the truth, or that this is the absolute. These answers are a ghostly conception, mere shadows of baseless delusions. Why not work deeply enough in meditation to reach the bottom of Mind-Essence? The outcome of this honest, hard work is attainment.

When one attains reality, one actually realizes the truth of all beings. He can prove it by his attitude toward "self-entity" and "self-limited ideas." He knows then that there is no ego entity, that all forms of objectivity are void, existing only in terms of relativity. A person may easily free himself of egoism in ethical life and may even consider himself unselfish in materialistic desire, but if he cannot listen to the opinions of others and insists on conquering the world with his own ideas, he is still an egoistic monster.

Zen realization must be manifested in two ways: rejection of an ego substance, and recognition of the voidness of all forms of objectivity. In a koan, one monk says, "The flag is moving." Another replies, "The wind is moving." The former clings to the entity of the flag. The latter has a broader view, but does not understand true emptiness. The Sixth Patriarch answers them, "The flag is not moving. The wind is not moving. The mind is moving." If you think the patriarch mentioned mind as a psychological phenomenon, you are entangled in self-limiting ideas.

When Yokadaishi said, "If you live in this Zen, you can leave hell in your dreams of yesterday, and make your own paradise wherever you stand . . . ," he did not mean that an enlightened man can ignore the law of causation. A person creates his own hell in which to suffer, and no one can save him but himself.

Some religious workers are in the business of selling people the idea that their sins can be wiped out by another. This was as widely practiced in Yokadaishi's day as in ours, so he warns such peddlers to beware of the myths they are creating. Those who speak untruth in this world, bishops or archbishops, reverends or right-reverends, are making a hell here and now.

> The minute you attain Buddha's Zen,
> The six noble deeds and ten thousand good actions are already
>   complete within you.
> In your dream there are six paths,
> But when you awake, they will be reduced to nothingness.

Buddha's Zen was transmitted first to Maha-Kasyapa[3] from heart to heart. There is no record in the Sutras about this inner teaching, but one whose meditation is mature receives the same genealogical wisdom. For this reason, Zen lives vividly through human experiences, transcending all scriptures and sectarian doctrines. Yokadaishi called Zen *Tathagata-dhyana*[4] in this work. Later Chinese masters named Zen the *Patriarch's Dhyana*.

[3] Maha-Kasyapa: a disciple of Buddha and first to receive the Lamp of Dharma, which was later transmitted in a direct line through Bodhi-Dharma, the patriarchs, etc.
[4] Tathagata-dhyana (Sanskrit): enlightened meditation.

A name is nothing but a symbol and can never be the thing it stands for. In the future, Americans may use a new name for their attainment. What I say about Zen is my own, nor can it be yours until you reach your own realization.

What are the six noble deeds? They are *Dana* (charity); *Sila* (keeping the precepts); *Ksanti* (perseverance); *Virya* (striving); *Dhyana* (meditation); and *Prajna* (wisdom).

What are the six paths? They are *Naraka* (hell); *Preta* (hungry devil); *Tiryag-yoni* (animal mind); *Asura* (fighting devil); *Manusya* (human being); and *Deva* (superior man).

Many people recognize these stages as having true existence, but to a Zen student they are nothing but shades of dualistic thought that vanish in the light of realization.

> No sin, no happiness, no loss, and no gain.
> Do not try to seek these things in Mind-Essence.
> For a long time you have not wiped the dust from your mirror,
> Now is the time for you to see its brilliance precisely.

No serious mind can think of sin and bliss in the old way any longer. Realization erases these ideas completely. These are idle concerns for a Zen student.

In his *Song of Meditation*, Hakuin said:

> From the very beginning you are Buddha. As there is no ice apart from water, so there is no Buddha outside our fellow beings. Although it is always within them, people fail to perceive the truth and search afar for it. They suffer thirst and do not see the fountain near at hand. They are in poverty and forget that they are heirs to boundless wealth. You say that you are suffering. You suffer only because of your own ignorance. Awake from your ignorant dream! The errors of the past will no longer harass you. Where is hell? You left it in yesterday's dream. Where is paradise? You are standing in it.

Your Mind-Essence is bright from the very beginning. This is the day to see it clearly. This is the moment to begin your work.

> Who thinks non-thinking and who recognizes non-existence?
> If it is really non-existence, you cannot think of it.

Ask a robot whether he is happy or not.
As long as you aim to become Buddha,
No matter how you strive, you will never be one.

Do these stanzas seem difficult? Remember that Zen can be realized but never explained. In your meditation you may already have experienced non-thinking. At this moment your "Mind-Mirror" is wiped and polished so thoroughly that there is not even a trace of brilliance remaining. But suppose you hear a dog bark? You visualize a running dog. You think of your pet dog. Then the train of thought passes in front of your nose endlessly. You cannot blame the dog for barking, nor your ears for receiving the sound. But why do you carry it as second thought? If, however, you think you are entering *Samadhi*, you are already out of it. When you count your breath, only count it. When you meditate on your koan, only meditate on it. In meditation you train yourself to carry the one subject of meditation; similarly, in daily life do one thing at a time without carrying unnecessary second thought.

Yokadaishi says, "Ask a robot whether he is happy or not." I can hear you complain, "Is Zen going to compel me to become a robot?" Do you wish to suffer, filling your mind with illusions? Do you know nothing of the joy of giving thoughts enough room in which to stretch themselves and grow? A Zen student has more time to enjoy life because he allows himself to think or to do one thing at a time, and does not block the flow of inner wisdom with the trash of delusions.

"As long as you aim to become Buddha, no matter how you strive, you will never be one." If you cannot find it where you stand, where do you expect to wander in search of it?

Do not cling to the four elements.
Drink and eat according to your true nature.
Things are transient; therefore, they are in a state of emptiness.
This is Buddha's realization.

Buddhism does not see mind and body as two different things. When it refers to the four elements, earth, water, fire, and air, it does not mean only the elements of the material world, but also the conditions of the mind as psychological phenomena. In Pali these four elements are called *pathavi* (solidity), *apo* (cohesion), *tejo* (radiability), and *vayu* (movability). Zen does not cling to these elements but instead lives in Mind-Essence leaving behind both mind and body. A Zen student "drinks or eats," that is, he lives his everyday life according to his own true nature.

To illustrate the third and fourth lines of this stanza, let's examine Tosotsu's koan from the *Gateless Gate*. "First, in studying Zen the aim is to see one's own true nature. Now where is your true nature? Second, when one realizes one's own true nature, one will be free from birth and death. Now, when you shut the light from your eyes, and become a corpse, how can you free yourself? Third, if you free yourself from birth and death, you should know where you are. Now, your body separates into four elements, where are you?"

Do not think of good or bad with your mind and body. Forget that you have a mind and body. Make the present moment the only true life you have. If an idea disturbs you, think of the impermanency of worldly things. When the illusions of individual entity vanish, the gate of true meditation will open. With empty hands and an empty mind you can meet your true self. Who said there exists Buddha's realization? Do not be cheated by Yokadaishi or anyone else. Find it out for yourself.

> A true disciple of Buddha speaks the ultimate truth.
> If you do not agree with what I say, you are free to discuss it.
> You must remember, however, that Buddhism is concerned with
>   the root of truth,
> Not with the branches or leaves.

What is the ultimate truth? Yokadaishi says that all things are transient and ultimately empty, and once this is seen there is realization. Southern Buddhists express the ultimate truth with three Pali words, *anicca*, *dukkha*, and *anatta*. *Anicca* expresses impermanence, your mind, your body, and the world you live in. One does not realize this fact, and so clings to what he likes. When he cannot hold it, he suffers, and this is known as *dukkha*. Life is an eternal flow. If you cannot hold even the mind and body you use, how can you expect to cling to other things and hold them? "Not I" is represented by *anatta*. When you understand these three characteristics, you will come to the real "I"—your true self.

Northern Buddhists express these fundamentals of Buddhism by 1) admitting the impermanence of all things; 2) denying the existence of individual soul; and 3) aiming at ultimate reality (Nirvana).[5]

When Yokadaishi said, "If you do not agree with what I say, you are free to discuss it," he was not inviting argument for the sake of debate. You cannot convince others of Zen through argument. No matter how cleverly logical you may be in cornering your opponent, you cannot give him enlightenment unless he opens his own eyes to attain it. You may clear his doubts by reasoning, but he must reach the root by himself.

> Most people do not recognize the mani-jewel, the gem of wisdom.
> It is hidden in the secret place of Tathagata awaiting discovery and attainment.
> The six senses and the six worlds interweave making life as it is.
> It is an illusion as a whole, yet nothing exists to be called illusion.
> The perfect light of this mani-jewel, the gem of wisdom, illuminates humanity.
> It has neither color nor form, nor has it non-color and non-form.

The mani-jewel is a legendary gem of old India that fulfills all desires of its possessor. Buddhists work for desirelessness, treasuring calmness and contentment and looking forward to the highest wisdom and moral perfection. Yokadaishi uses "mani-jewel" metaphorically, saying that it can be found in "the secret

[5]Nirvana: synonymous with enlightenment, but is not a negative condition as many suppose, nor a condition of non-existence, nor is it to be sought outside of Samsara, the world of birth and death.

place of Tathagata." But Tathagata has nothing to do with time or place.

Your eyes create the world of color and form; your ears, the world of sound; your nose, the world of odor; your tongue, the world of taste; and your brain, the world of thought. The sixfold function is manifested as the numerous images of the moon that may appear on ponds, lakes, or the sea, or the many waves that may rise and fall on the selfsame body of the great ocean.

Everything appears through contact of subjective and objective elements, and you recognize and name them in terms of relativity. This is the performance of the mani-jewel, which subjectively you call your true self, and objectively, Buddha-nature.

> Clarify the five kinds of vision, and acquire the five powers.
> It is possible only through Zen meditation, which goes beyond speculation.
> One can see the images in the mirror naturally.
> To hold the reflection of the moon on the water is impossible.

The five kinds of vision are the physical, heavenly, Prajna, Dharma, and Buddha-vision. The five powers are faith, energy, memory, meditation, and wisdom. One attains these five types of vision and power through unification with Mind-Essence, where they are facets of the same gem of wisdom.

Everyone knows that the physical eye must have light in order to see, and that even then sight is not to be relied upon implicitly.

Modern science has developed the heavenly eye in the telescope and the microscope, bringing into the range of vision things that could not otherwise be seen.

The Prajna or wisdom eye views the world without desire, and the person who possesses it can avoid entangling, dualistic thoughts.

The Dharma eye is the eye of higher wisdom in the world of discrimination. A Zen student who has sound knowledge of modern science and philosophy, and is well acquainted with other religions and the cultures of many lands so that he may view the condition of other beings with sympathy and tolerance, is using the vision of Dharma.

The Buddha eye is the perfect eye. When a student attains complete realization, he sees the world in truth as it is in reality. This is the eye of perfect compassion, free of all defilement.

The five powers are self-evident. Faith allows one to stand firmly in truth; energy is necessary to continue the climb; memory increases and enriches knowledge; meditation guards a person's calmness, which is the source of the fifth power: Prajna, the wisdom of emancipation.

Yokadaishi often speaks of the "mirror." This mirror belongs to each one of us, ready to use. It is easy to recognize the images it seems to contain, but the moment you think you have them, they vanish. Who can hold "the reflection of the moon on the water"?

The five kinds of vision are inherent in Zen realization, and the five powers manifest as you practice Zen in your everyday life. The secret is to live every minute in Zen. Receive, use, and then forget what you see in your mirror, knowing it is only a reflection with no self-entity.

> A Zen student should walk alone at all times.
> Those who have attained, tread the same road of Nirvana.
> Each of them is natural in manner, and clean and contented of heart.
> Since not one of them is concerned with special attraction, no one pays him special attention.

In the Old Testament, Psalms 10:1, David complains, "Why standest thou afar off, O Lord? Why hidest thou thyself in times of trouble?" No matter how closely God approaches David, they are still two and not one. A Zen student worships no god, observes no orthodox rites, does not look forward to a future abode, nor has a soul to be cared for by anyone else. He walks freely, unburdened by dogmatic and theological postulation, knowing that as he masters his situation, wherever he stands is the land of truth.

His Zen training and meditation are for nothing but his perfect emancipation.

He walks alone in Mind-Essence. Who calls it the road of Nirvana? He has no such road ahead of him. He goes ahead step-by-step naturally and wisely. His heart is clean and he is always contented. He works hard; therefore, he is strong. He is not worried about his appearance, and so attracts no attention. He lives among men quietly and easily.

> The followers of Buddha speak of their poverty.
> The simplicity of their living may be called poor, but not their Zen.
> A monk's gown, torn and mended, shows the world his poverty;
> His Zen, unseen by others, is the treasure beyond all value.

A Chinese Zen master was once asked to name the most valuable treasure in the world. He answered that it was the head of a dead cat. When questioned as to his reason for this answer, he replied, "Because no one can name the price." How would you like to become the head of a dead cat? Zen students! Philosophers! Occult students! Metaphysicians! Theologians! Atheists! They are all noisy, living cats with their price clearly written on their foreheads! A true seeker of enlightenment cannot display his value.

> No matter how much it is used, the priceless treasure never deteriorates.
> It may be given freely to others who need it.
> The three bodies of Buddha and the four kinds of wisdom are completely contained in it.
> The eight sorts of emancipation and the six miraculous powers are merely impressions of the same seal.

Takuan, a Japanese Zen master, wrote a poem of eight Chinese characters, which reads:

> Not twice this day
> Inch time foot gem.

In a free translation into English these words mean
> This day will not come again.
> Each minute is worth a priceless gem.

The three bodies of Buddha are considered to be the Dharma-body, the attainment body, and the transformation body. Each one of us has the Dharma-body; through realization it becomes the body of attainment; in our daily action and associations with others it produces the transformation body.

The four kinds of wisdom are the mirror intuition, the intuition of identity, the clear perception of relations, and the knowledge of work.

The eight-fold emancipation is emancipation by materialism; emancipation by idealism; emancipation by aestheticism; emancipation by relativity; emancipation by spiritualism; emancipation by Hinayana thought; emancipation by distinction of Hinayana and Mahayana teaching; emancipation by *prajnaparamita*, the understanding of emptiness in Mahayana teaching.

The six miraculous powers are geographical, visual, auditory, fatal, psychic, and purificatory.

There is no need to memorize these lists. Everything is contained in your realization. When you attain enlightenment, you are like a person who possesses a seal. You may make many impressions on varying materials, the color and the shade may also vary, but each is made by the one seal of ultimate wisdom.

The priceless treasure belongs to everyone. Each of us is a part of Dharma-kaya, but how can we realize it unless we meditate and obtain the fruit of our striving? This is the body of attainment, but attainment does not denote static conclusion. It is the pure force used to serve humanity, which is called the body of transformation. When you hear the sound of one hand, you have mirror-intuition. When you can put out a light one thousand miles away, you are practicing your intuition of identity. When you can tell me whether the man you meet is your younger brother or older brother, you have a clear perception of relations.

When you can show me how you enter an object, such as a stick of incense, and pay homage to all the Buddhas, you are proving your knowledge of doing work in Zen. As for emancipation, what a foolish idea to make it eightfold! The blue skies have no limit! We merely designate the floating clouds as being here or there.

Your geographical miracle is accomplished when you bring me some snow from the top of Mt. Whitney; your auditory miracle when you hear the song of angels in the thirty-third heaven; your fatal miracle when you know where you were when Gautama Buddha was born in India; your psychic miracle when you know the one whose servants are the present Buddha, past Buddhas, and future Buddhas; and your miracle of purification when you avoid all evil thoughts and actions to develop good thoughts and right actions, not only for yourself but for all with whom you associate. Miracles! What nonsense! Just use each moment of the law of causation.

> The excellent student of Zen goes directly to the ultimate truth.
> The fair or good ones like to learn from others but have no steady faith.
> Once you strip off the tattered clothing of prejudice you will see your true self.
> How can you wander around in outward striving?

Muso Kokushi, a Japanese Zen master, once spoke of the three types of students. First, there were those who threw off all entangling conditions to apply themselves wholeheartedly to the study of Zen; second, there came those who were not so single-minded, seeking a solution in books or other activities; the third and lowest group was made up of students who repeated the words of Buddha or the patriarchs instead of digging for the treasure within themselves.

If Zen is not a teaching that can settle the matter once and for all, then a lay student has little chance of becoming a first class disciple. Zen belongs to the abrupt school of Buddhism. You may spend a long time mining for your inner treasure, but the moment you unearth it, you will instantly see its brilliance. Those who insist that you will find only a fragment at a time are like those who would carry out the darkness before lighting a room.

You can forget your worries of the past and future to live only in the peaceful present. Each moment contains an opportunity for you to be an excellent student of Zen.

> Some may slander or argue against Zen.
> They are playing with fire, trying to burn the heavens in vain.
> A true student of Zen will take their words as sweet dewdrops.
> Forgetting even this sweetness when he enters the region of non-thinking.

A Zen student will find few people who agree with his beliefs or understand his effortless effort. Other sects of Buddhism decree that a student must go through many stages even to hope to attain enlightenment in a future incarnation, and other religions will find many points of difference on which to hang their arguments. Since argument never convinced anyone, let alone enlightened him, a Zen student will avoid all fruitless discussion, helping others whenever he can without seeking assistance for himself. He knows where his treasure lies and how to use it.

One night many years ago a blind man, visiting a friend, was offered a lantern to carry home with him. "I do not need a lantern," he said, "darkness and light are the same to me." "I know you do not need a lantern to find your way home," his friend replied, "but if you do not take it, someone else may run into you. You must take it." The blind man took the lantern, but before he had gone very far, someone walked straight into him. "Look where you're going," the blind man exclaimed. "Can't you see this lantern?" "Your candle has burned out," the stranger answered.

Always be sure your candle is burning, both for your own safety and for the sake of others.

> I observe abusive words as virtuous action,
> And consider the abuser as one of my good teachers.

Since my feeling is neither for nor against the abuser,
Why should I express the two powers of perseverance, the knowl-
    edge of the unborn and the love of all beings?

Yokadaishi not only teaches the negative attitude towards slan-
derers, he even tells us to regard the abuser positively. People may
confess their sins to God, but may not care to have others criticize
their minor faults. Much as they may admit deserving such crit-
icism, it is painful for them. A Zen student not only listens, but
accepts critical words with gratitude.

When Yokadaishi asks, "Why should I express the two powers
of perseverance," he means to avoid fussing about "reasons," and
worrying about "why" and "because." When there is no cognition of "I" or "he," there is no relativity of "I" and "not I." This is
the knowledge of the unborn. Every Bodhisattva or Zen student
loves all sentient beings irrespective of appearance or condition.
He does not fall into the trap of dualism, saying, "This man has
slandered me. I shall be especially loving to him." His knowledge
and love are expressed in all he thinks and does as naturally as the
sun shines upon the earth or a white cloud floats across the blue
sky.

One who attains Zen must acquire its eloquence.
Meditation and wisdom must have their full brilliance un-
    clouded by an idea of emptiness.
Such an accomplishment is not limited to the few.
The Buddhas, countless as the sands of the Ganges, are all witness
    to this fact.

There are four kinds of eloquence. First, the eloquence of
Dhamma permits you to express the ultimate wisdom once you
attain enlightenment. A single act may adequately express your
interpretation of inner wisdom when you gain realization. Second is the eloquence of reason. Buddhism is a religion of reason.
If your eyes are clear, you should have no difficulty in reporting
what you see. Third is the eloquence of utterance. Zen students
should use their words economically. People waste words be-

cause they lack concentration. If silence is golden, it would seem that there are entirely too many silver pieces in circulation these days. Fourth is the eloquence of compassion. When you have learned to lead a pure, unselfish life, your words will become kind and powerful.

Beginners in meditation often cling one-sidedly to an erroneous idea of emptiness, refusing positive action or remaining coldly distant from the world. Once they have experienced true emptiness, however, their love is greater than that of even the kindest unenlightened person.

This accomplishment is not limited to a few people, as the innumerable Buddhas (enlightened ones) will bear witness.

> The fearless thought of Zen is like the mighty roar of the lion,
> Striking terror in the hearts of other beasts.
> Even the king of elephants will run away forgetting his pride.
> Courageous students alone, like the dragon, hear the roar with
>   calm pleasure.

When a Zen student comes for *Sanzen*,[6] he strikes the bell twice without the slightest fear. In that moment he transcends both birth and death; he is beyond space and time. What he says now comes directly from his own Buddha-nature and is called the "roar of the lion." This does not mean that he shouts. He is not an empty radio turned on at full volume. His speech is the result of his hard work, and even though I may reject his answer, his calmness is unbroken. Sometimes a student will bring a bag full of answers, trying one after another to fit the question, but he is like a peddler in a vain attempt to please a customer. Instead of reaching the palace of wisdom, he will return to his old alley of blind faith with all the stray cats that symbolize superstition.

In Asia it is said that, "To study Zen requires the spirit of a hero." Zen will never appeal to the masses. In all ages, students of Zen have been intelligent, compassionate, and courageous,

[6]Sanzen (from Chinese *San-Ch'an*): to study Zen, especially the examination of a student by a teacher.

then when they attain realization, they help each person according to individual need. They are not quacks prescribing one panacea for all ailments, but wise physicians assisting each person to cure his particular illness. They have accomplished their meditation, and their one aim is to aid all sentient beings to achieve theirs.

> Zen students journey by land and sea, across rivers and over mountains,
> Visiting monasteries and receiving personal guidance from teachers.
> I also followed the way, reaching Sokei, where I met my master and received Dhamma.
> Now I know my true being has nothing to do with birth and death.

It took Yokadaishi many years to reach Sokei. He had to cross the rivers of speculation, the sea of intellectuality, where many contemporary scholars had drifted off their course never to reach the shores of Nirvana, and finally he had to climb the mountains of meditation to attain self-realization. The Sixth Patriarch did not bestow Dhamma on Yoka, he only affirmed the latter's attainment.

Although many of the koans and Zen stories are woven around traveling or secluded monks, nothing will be achieved by our clinging to and imitating these outward circumstances. A Zen student is neither a misanthropist nor a misogynist, so there is no need to shut himself up in some forest cabin or to avoid the opposite sex. He just controls his own environment and masters his situation wherever he stands.

In order to know the author of this poem intimately, we must remember the last line of the stanza, "Now I know my true being has nothing to do with birth and death." This is your koan. How can you free yourself from birth and death? What is your true being? No, no! Do not think about it! Just gaze at it closely.

> A Zen student walks in Zen and sits in Zen.
> Whether in speech and action, or silence and inaction, his body always dwells in peace.

He smiles, facing the sword that takes his life.
He keeps his poise even at the moment of death, nor can drugs
   alter his calm.

Meditation is practiced in four ways. First, your mind and
body are still. This is the source of all of your Zen actions. Second, your body is still but your mind moves, as in reading or listening to a lecture. Third, your mind is still but your body moves,
as in walking. Fourth, your mind and body move as you do your
work in daily life. Thus, at each moment a good Zen student experiences the Mind-Essence at ease.

Our great teacher, Sakyamuni, met Dipankara Buddha[7] many
   millions of years ago, and accepted his Dharma.
Ever since, he is master of *Ksanti*, perseverance, life after life.

Some people may be interested in past lives, but Zen students
see life as an eternal presence. Stories of "incarnation" insinuate
the idea of individual personality distorting the vision of truth
seekers. When you extend time and narrow space, you will see
Buddha Sakyamuni receiving Dhamma from Dipankara Buddha many millions of years ago, but when you extend space and
limit time, you will see *Ksanti*, or perseverance, mastering human affairs. It is the actual business of the present moment. Until
students of occultism understand this and come to their senses,
spiritual gold-diggers will strike it rich here and abroad.

Man is born many times, so he dies many times.
Life and death continue endlessly.
If he realizes the true meaning of unborn,
He will transcend both gladness and grief.

He lives alone in a mountain hut
Among the old pine trees,
Meditating comfortably
And living peacefully.

[7]Dipankara Buddha: one of the early Buddhas before the time of Gautama Buddha.

Those who understand Dhamma always act naturally.
Most people in the world live in *samskrita*,[8] but Zen students live
in *asamskrita*.[9]
Those who give something to others to receive something in re-
turn,
Are shooting arrows heavenwards.
The arrow, which was shot against heaven, returns to the earth.
When striving and gaining are balanced, nothing remains.
Aimless striving is quite different,
It opens the gate of truth leading to the garden of Tathagata.
A true Zen student ignores the branches and leaves until he
reaches the root.
It is like the image of the moon reflected in the water of a jade
bowl.
The real beauty of the mani-gem, treasure of emancipation, I
now know . . .
I and others are benefited eternally.

We devote ourselves to meditation in order to reach the root of
the teaching. Do not ask me any foolish questions. First of all find
out who you really are. The reflection of the moon on the water
is beautiful, but the moon itself is not there nor is its beauty lingering in the sky.

The moon rises above the river, the wind plays softly in the pines
on the shore
All night long. What is the meaning of this serenity?
You must see the precepts of Buddha-nature vividly imprinted.
Dew, fog, cloud, and mist clothe the original man in full.

The preceding stanza is a koan. You must work hard to catch
a glimpse of it. If you think that I am hiding something from you,
you are the guilty one. I am concealing nothing from you.

A begging bowl once conquered dragons and a staff pacified fighting tigers.

[8]Samskrita: subject to causation, the world of birth and death.
[9]Asamskrita: not subject to causation, the world of birthlessness and deathlessness.

The staff had six rings on top whose tinkling called people from
   their dreams.
The bowl and the staff are not mere symbols of the teaching,
But Tathagata's actual work remaining in the world.

Legend says that Buddha Sakyamuni conquered dragons making them so small that they stayed in his begging bowl. With his
staff, a Zen master once stopped the fighting of two tigers and so
saved them from killing each other. These stories are neither symbols nor miracles. When you attain the mani-gem, you too can
perform the same deeds.

Where are the burdens of egoism you have carried for many
years? Where are the dualistic ideas that fight continuously in
your mind? Look! The moon rises above the river of *Samsara*.[10]
The wind plays the melody of Buddha-Dhamma in the pines on
the shore. What is the meaning of this serenity? Now you have
no burden of egoism nor discord of dualism. Is this a miracle?
Anyone can experience it if he has the courage to break his delusions and face himself as he had always been beyond time and
space.

An ideal Zen student neither seeks the true nor avoids the untrue.
He knows that these are merely dualistic ideas that have no form.
Non-form is neither empty nor not empty.
It is the true form of Buddha's wisdom.

To assist you in the interpretation of the stanza above, I shall
paraphrase a portion of *Shin-jin-mei*, a poem written by the
Third Patriarch in China. "Truth is like vast space without en-
trance or exit. There is nothing more nor nothing less. Foolish
people limit themselves, covering their eyes, but truth is never
hidden. Some attend lectures trying to grasp truth in the words
of others. Some accumulate books and try to dig truth from them.
They are all wrong. A few of the wiser ones may learn meditation
in their effort to reach an inner void. They choose the void rather

[10]Samsara: the world of birth and death.

than outer entanglements, but it is still the same old dualistic trick. Just think non-thinking if you are a true Zen student. There you do not know anything, but you are with everything. There is no choice nor preference, and dualism will vanish by itself. But if you stop moving and hold quietness, that quietness is ever in motion. If children make a noise, you will scold them loudly so that the situation is worse than before. Just forget and ignore the noise, and you will attain peace of mind. When you forget your liking and disliking, you will get a glimpse of oneness. The serenity of this middle way is quite different from the inner void."

> The mind mirror illumines all ingenuously.
> Its penetrating, limitless rays reach everywhere in the universe.
> Without exception everything is reflected in this mirror.
> The whole universe is a gem of light beyond the terms of in and
> out.

Here is another portion of *Shin-jin-mei* to interpret the preceding stanza: "Zen transcends time and space. Ten thousand years are nothing but a thought after all. What you have seen is what you had in the whole world. If your thought transcends time and space, you will know that the smallest thing is large and the largest thing is small, that being is non-being and non-being is being. Without such experience you will hesitate to do anything. If you can realize that one is many, and many are one, your Zen will be completed.

"Faith and Mind-Essence are not separate from each other. You will see only the 'not two.' The 'not two' is the faith. The 'not two' is the Mind-Essence. There is no other way but silence to express it properly. This silence is not the past. This silence is not the present. This silence is not the future."

> When a Zen student sees emptiness one-sidedly, he is likely to
> ignore the law of causation.
> He will then live aimlessly with evil thoughts and wrong actions.

His idea is morbid as he denies the existence of anything, but ad-
mits an entity of emptiness.
To escape drowning he has thrown himself into the fire.

To "see emptiness one-sidedly" is to give another name to relativity, phenomenality, or nothingness. When Buddhism denies
the existence of everything, this of course includes the existence
of emptiness. There is order, and there is the law of causation.
The use of the word "emptiness" implies that which cannot be
spoken.

He who rejects delusions to search for truth
May achieve skill in discrimination,
But such a student will never reach enlightenment
Because he mistakes his enemy for his own dear child.

Some Christians admire an angel but hate a devil. Some Con-
fucians pine for the ancient kingdom but complain of the present
government. All of them attempt to take hold of the true by aban-
doning the false. They struggle endlessly, but never attain true
peacefulness. Zen students who try to reach truth by rejecting
delusions are making the same mistake. Scientists reduce matter
to atoms, then divide the atom as they divided the molecule.
They are driven to the dilemma that matter is infinitely divisible,
which is inconceivable, or that there is a limit to its divisibility,
which is also inconceivable. It is the same with time and space.
When we analyze matter, we find nothing but force, a force im-
pressed upon our organs of sense, or a force resisting our organs
of action. Who shall tell us what force is? When we turn from
physics to psychology, we come upon mind and consciousness.
Here we find greater puzzles than before.

We must not postulate the true outside the untrue. We must
see holiness transmuting unholy conditions. We must establish
the kingdom of heaven here and now. The terms given by science
and philosophy are based upon dualistic delusions, no matter

what skill there is in discrimination. Do not become enchanted by such expressions as "God within," or "I am That," but experience the *Samadhi* where there is no god, within or without, where there is no this, no that, no I, and no you. Then you may use the Christian terms freely, if you like, and say, "God not in the world is a false God, and the world not in God is unreality." Until that time, learn silence and work on constantly in silence, to see clearly what the mind is.

> Man misses the spiritual treasure and loses the proper merit
> Because he depends on dualistic thinking and neglects the essence of mind.
> To pass through the gate of Zen one must correct this error.
> Then he can attain the wisdom to enter the palace of Nirvana.

Buddhists often refer to the "seven treasures," which are faith, perseverance, listening, humility, precepts, self-surrender, and meditation and wisdom. (Meditation and wisdom are considered one—inner cultivation and outer illumination.) To acquire these seven treasures one must first of all see one's own Mind-Essence clearly, just as Aladdin had first to find the lamp before he could produce other wonders.

Wobaku, a Chinese Zen master, once said, "Buddhas and sentient beings both grow out of One Mind, and there is no reality other than this Mind. . . . Only because we seek it outwardly in a world of form, the more we seek the farther away it moves from us. To make Buddha seek after himself, or to make the Mind take hold of itself is impossible to the end of eternity. We do not realize that as soon as our thoughts cease and all attempts at forming ideas are forgotten, the Buddha is revealed before us."

> The true student of Zen carries the sword of Prajna (the wisdom of emancipation),
> The blade is so sharp that one feels the searing flame around it.
> It cuts away the delusions of non-Buddhist thought as well as the haughty pride of heavenly devils.

Sometimes the student preaches like a thunderstorm;
Sometimes he pours the gentle rain of loving kindness.
He walks like the king of the elephants, yet always loves other
beings.
He teaches five students of different nature, leading them to Buddhahood, although they come to him through the three different gates.

"Heavenly devils" are those who call themselves Zen masters
or those who wear the robes of various religious sects, and think
that by so doing they have been equally invested with some divine
right to direct the lives of others. Pride is one of the most subtle
and insidious evils of all, appearing in many forms. Only the student who has accomplished Prajna has any right to lead others.

The five types of students are those who enter Buddhahood by
realizing the four noble truths (*Çravaka*); the twelve *nidanas*[11]
(Pratyeka-Buddha); or the six *paramitas* (*Bodhisattva*); some students are uncertain; and others fit none of these categories. Even
so, the true student of Zen guides each according to his understanding until he attains enlightenment.

The precious grass of the Himalayas is the only kind in the
meadow.
Cows that graze there give the best milk from which is made the
richest cheese.
Zen students partake of teaching always as pure.
When human character is purified, it is the character of all
beings;
When the law of humanity is completed, it is the law of the uni-
verse.
One moon is reflected on many waters;
Innumerable reflections are nothing but the image of one moon.
The Dharma-kaya of all Buddhas becomes my inner being;
My inner being is unified with Tathagata.
One stage of meditation contains all other stages completely;

[11] Nidana: the process of karma relation.

The Essence of Mind is not limited by color, form, thought, or
    activity.
A snap of the fingers and eight thousand gates of the teaching are
    established.
A wink of the eye and countless ages of time have vanished.
Innumerable names and categories have nothing to do with my
    realization.

"One touch of nature makes the whole world kin." All things
return to one, and one operates in all things. When you pass one
koan, you have passed all koans. It is your own fault if you are
entangled by the next one. Realization has no color, no form, no
psychological movement, and no action of dualistic tendency.

You cannot praise nor blame realization.
Like the sky, truth has no bounds.
Wherever you stand, it surrounds you.
When you seek it, you cannot reach it;
Your hand cannot hold it, nor your mind exclude it.
When you no longer seek it, it is with you.
In silence, you speak it loudly; in speech you manifest its silence.
Thus the gate of compassion opens wide to the benefit of all
    beings.

When you begin to study Zen, you aim to attain realization.
Your motive is good insofar as motive is concerned, but in your
meditation you should aim at nothing. You may aim at realization to encourage yourself when you are not meditating, but beware of clinging entanglements. Encouragement is one thing,
meditation is another. Do not mix them up. Carry your meditation as the eternal present, and saturate your everyday life in it.

When a person asks me what branch of Buddhism I studied,
I tell him about *Mahaprajna*,[12] the root of the teaching.
Without Mahaprajna, though you know right and wrong, you are
    beyond truth.
With the root of the teaching, wherever you go is the land of truth.
I studied Mahaprajna for many, many lives;

[12] Mahaprajna (Sanskrit): great wisdom, the wisdom of the Buddhas.

This statement is neither to deceive you nor trick you.
I was told to spread the teaching;
The order came from Buddha through the generations.
The Lamp of Wisdom was first transmitted to Mahakasyapa,
Then genealogically through twenty-eight patriarchs.
Bodhi-Dharma, the patriarch of India, came to this country across the seas.
My teacher, who works in Sokei, received his robe
To become the Sixth Patriarch in this land, as you have heard.
Who knows how many generations will carry the teaching in the future?

Buddhism is the teaching of self-enlightenment. No God or gods will help you to realize the truth. The power of realization within you is called Mahaprajna, meaning great wisdom. This is the root of the teaching, the source of all streams of Buddhistic thought. Those who speculate, reading scriptures or clinging to creeds and dogmas, wander far from realization. Ethical deeds and kind actions may be praised, but they are without real value until they spring from Mahaprajna.

When Yoka speaks of having studied for many, many lives, he is not referring to innumerable incarnations. When he attained his Zen, he lost his delusions to become one with the vast ocean of wisdom whose waves of Buddhas and patriarchs were also his. The brilliancy of Mahaprajna illumines all beings; Buddhas and patriarchs reflect this brilliance one to the other.

Yoka gives a brief history of Zen, then wonders how future generations will carry the teaching. To discover or to ignore the latent Mahaprajna is the individual choice of each person.

The true never exists alone, and the false never exists alone.
When the idea of existence and non-existence vanishes, the idea of emptiness and non-emptiness disappears.
The Sutra gives twenty names to emptiness, each showing you the one body of Buddha-nature.
The mind rises and contacts the outer world, thus delusions appear.

Subjectivity and objectivity are like dust on the surface of a mirror.
When the mirror is free of dust, it shines brightly.
If no mind rises, there is no contact, no delusion . . . only the
true nature of man appears.

Yoka is warning us not to postulate true and false. Without
dualism one can easily reach the truth, but one must experience
it in meditation. The result of meditation is beyond words and
ideas. The names of emptiness are like a list of drugs. If you are
well and strong, you are not interested in them. Many teachers
seek to hold or to mystify a student by using the various desig-
nations of good or evil built up through the ages. If you wish to
make a business of teaching, then memorize the names, but if
you want emancipation for yourself and others, give up the drug
business and practice Zen meditation.

It is sad to live in the time when Dhamma is not practiced and
evil thoughts grow.
The people cannot accept true teaching and cannot discipline
themselves.
They live far from wisdom, clinging to wrong ideas.
Evil is strong and disciples are weak, fear and hatred are spread-
ing.
Even though they hear of the intuitive teaching of Tathagata,
They desire to crush it under their heels.

There are three processes of Buddhism to establish the teaching in contemporary minds: first, the teaching must be well
understood; second, it must be strictly practiced; third, it must be
precisely realized and actualized.

The stanza above refers to the Sutra in which Buddha pre-
dicted that one thousand years after his death the people would
learn Dhamma, practice it, and attain its fruits; for the next thousand years people would learn the teaching, and some might
practice it, but would not continue and not attain its fruits; for the
following ten thousand years people might hear about Dhamma,
but they would not practice it, so of course they will not attain

enlightenment. A person chooses his own era . . . accuracy, imitation, or degeneration. He may study for years only to accumulate knowledge (his age of degeneration), but if he is brave and sincere enough to concentrate his study of meditation, next week may be his era of imitation or accuracy.

Craving produces action affecting man's suffering.
It is useless to blame others when you reap what you have sown.
Those who do not wish to suffer in hell,
Should not slander the Wheel of Dhamma.

When Buddha taught the law of causation to his disciples, he said, "Actions are determined by ignorance; by action, consciousness is determined; by consciousness are determined name and shape; by name and shape the senses are determined; the senses determine contact; by contact, feeling is determined; by feeling, craving is determined; by craving, grasping is determined; grasping determines becoming; by becoming, birth is determined; by birth are age and death determined, sorrow, grief, woe, lamentation, and despair. Such is the arising of all this mass of ill."

Any Zen teacher will warn you that there is no equality without discrimination, and that there is no discrimination without equality, but few students understand this nuance of meaning.

It is a self-evident fact that each person, irrespective of attainment, is subject to the law of causation. If he would terminate his own suffering and help others as well, then let him work in accord with the law of the universe rather than strive to evade it.

No other trees grow in the forest of Chandana[13] wood;
For countless ages only lions have lived there,
Roaming freely in the silent, dark grove.
No birds and no other animals enter the forest,
Only the lion cubs follow the older beasts. . . .
Even the three-year-old roars loudly.

[13]Chandana (Sanskrit): sandalwood.

52			BUDDHISM AND ZEN

How can a yelping fox imitate the king of Dhamma?
Even though hundreds of monsters open their mouths, it will be
	in vain.

It is said in India that no inferior trees grow near a forest of
Chandana, so Buddhists use the name as a symbol of ultimate
wisdom. In this stanza, birds and beasts represent fame and glory.
Monks are indifferent to these in any form in any age. Only the
lion cubs can follow the older lions, and even they have learned
to roar while still young. A yelping fox may fool some with his
imitations, as a false teacher will use the words and rituals of true
teachings, but when he meets a real lion he will be helpless.

Zen doctrine is no subject for sentiment.
Doubts cannot be cleared by argument.
I stubbornly demand your silence
To save you from the pitfall of being and non-being.

Zen allows no student to waste his time even for a second. If
you have a koan, work on it; if you have no koan, just count your
breath. Do not acknowledge doubt. Just keep on meditating.
This is the only means of learning to walk the Middle Way.

Wrong is not always wrong, nor is right always right.
If you cling to fixed ideas, a tenth of an inch's difference will set
	you ten thousand miles away.
When she reaches the source, the infant female dragon enters
	Buddhahood;
When he fails to touch the essence, a learned disciple of Buddha
	suffers the tortures of hell.

The *Saddharma-pundarika-sutra* mentions an infant female
dragon that attained realization, and in the *Mahaparinirvana-
sutra* is found the story of Zensho, the learned disciple, who suf-
fered the tortures of hell. But why search the scriptures when we
witness such examples every day of our lives? Sex, age, and intellectuality have nothing to do with enlightenment.

From early youth I have accumulated the knowledge of Bud-
	dhism, studying the Sutras and Sastras.

I had no time to rest as I classified the terms of the teaching.
Like a man counting the grains of sand on the shore, I tired myself
    in vain.
I felt that Buddha scolded me as I read his words in the Sutra,
"Why name the price of your neighbor's treasure?"
For years I traveled in the wrong direction,
Like a prodigal son wandering from his home.

A Zen student must spend more time in meditation than he does in reading . . . even Zen books. Without your own experience you will be a stranger to Zen and a philosophical tramp. Find your own treasure.

A man whose character is wrongly developed seldom understands
    things correctly.
It is difficult for him to attain the abrupt wisdom of Tathagata.
Two classes of students seek emancipation for themselves, not for
    the love of sentient beings.
Worldly scholars have dualistic knowledge, but they lack Prajna,
    the wisdom of emancipation.

Confucius said, "By nature men are almost alike; by practice they are far apart." Those who love all sentient beings will meditate to save them, thereby developing their own character in Zen. The mind of Çravaka is ready to listen to an enlightened man, but only to eliminate its own suffering. Some study Zen to overcome weaknesses such as temper, cowardliness, and excitability. These are selfish students. The mind of Pratyeka-Buddha is also alert for study, but its motive is not altruistic. Non-Buddhistic scholars have dualistic knowledge, which makes them intellectual, but they lack Prajna and realize that their efforts will not bring mankind true happiness.

Those who are stupid and childish wander beyond realization.
When they see a closed fist, they assume there is something in it.
If you point your finger to the moon, they discuss the finger, not
    the moon.
Their thought never goes beyond the five senses as they play hide-
    and-seek in the material world.

When Zen opens its closed fist to show that there is nothing within, spiritual customers are lost. These people enjoy the intoxication of illusion, and knowing nothing, they recite the scriptures and attend the services with enthusiasm. They are idle dreamers, easily deluded, and their wrongly developed characters find the abrupt system of emancipation difficult to understand.

> The one who sees nothing but Mind-Essence is Tathagata himself.
> He should be called Avalokitesvara,[14] the one who sees the world clearly with wisdom and compassion.
> When one realizes the truth, he knows that karma hindrance does not exist as an entity.
> The one who knows not true emptiness worries about debts and credits.

Once you realize that nothing exists, everything being the manifestation of Mind-Essence, which is also free of being and non-being, you are Tathagata, the Enlightened One.

The Enlightened One has to pay his karmic debts just as anyone else does, but he does not worry about them nor does he contract new debts.

> The hungry man refuses the royal feast;
> How can the ill be cured when they turn from the good physician?

Is your hunger satisfied when another eats? Is your thirst quenched when another drinks? Are you rested when another sleeps? By whose efforts will you be enlightened?

> If you have the wisdom of Prajna, you can practice Zen in the world of desires.
> Like the lotus unconsumed by the fire, nothing can destroy your Zen.

[14] Avalokitesvara (Sanskrit): the Buddha of Compassion; in Chinese *Kwan-yin*; in Japanese *Kwannon*.

Although Yuse, a monk, once broke the main precepts, he went
    ahead, without faltering, to reach Nirvana;
The pure land, which he built, exists even now.
Buddha-Dhamma makes anyone fearless.
What a pity that stupid minds do not appreciate this fact!
They consider only the loss or gain within the precepts
Forgetting that they can still open the secret door of Tathagata
    unaided.
In ages past two monks broke the precepts.
Their chief monk, Upali, considered them hopeless in the light
    of his feeble understanding,
But Vimalakirti, a layman, cleared their clouds of doubt to realize
    truth as frost is melted in the warm sunshine.

A Zen student must pass through the world of desires. In India
a story is told of a lotus flower that bloomed in the midst of fire.
Like the lotus or like the phoenix, a Zen student will rise from the
ashes of his worldly desires and vain regrets, never turning from
his course toward enlightenment. He will pay his karmic debts
without question. The frost of his doubt is melted by the warm
sunshine of realization that illumines all beings.

The wonderful power of emancipation!
It is applied in countless ways . . . in limitless ways.
One should make four kinds of offering for this treasure.
If you mean to pay for it, a million gold pieces are not enough;
If you sacrifice everything you have, it will not cover your debt.
A few words from your realization are payment in full, even for
    debts of the remote past.

Some sincere students meditate morning and evening and at
any other leisure moment to attain emancipation. You have studied other religions and schools of philosophy hoping to free yourself from entanglement, and some of these have taken a part of
your familiar burden only in exchange for their own creeds and
dogmas. You must throw them all off at once!

Buddhism takes away unnecessary burdens and gives you
nothing in return. If you think you have attained anything in this

Zendo, drop it at the gate and go home with empty hands. There you will find yourself in an atmosphere of peace . . . this is your power of emancipation.

The four kinds of offering are clothes, bedding, food, and medicine. These are always given to a monk, but any man, who has the power of emancipation, owes his happiness not only to monks or teachers but to mankind and all sentient beings.

> Zen, superior among all teachings, is the Dharma king,
> As is proven by the attainment of countless Tathagatas.
> Now I know what the mani-gem is,
> I transmit it to anyone who receives it accordingly.

Although there is nothing to be termed great or small in Prajna, all people cherish comparative thoughts until they are enlightened; therefore, Yokadaishi says that the innumerable Tathagatas prove that Zen provides the most direct route to wisdom for those who are strong enough to undertake this path. Even though most people will avoid this steep, rocky course, those who follow it make the choice themselves . . . they are not chosen by a god, they are not accidentally a member of a favored race, nation, or creed. Such superficialities have nothing to do with Zen. Each one of you may become a Bodhisattva.

> In the eye of realization there is nothing to be seen.
> There is neither man nor Buddha;
> All things in the universe are mere bubbles on the sea.
> Sages and wise men disappear in a lightning flash.

Jews and Christians find it difficult to erase the idea of a god separate from man; although Buddhists know that Gautama Buddha was once a person like themselves, most of them cherish the idea of becoming a Buddha only in some future life. All are caught in the web of dualism, wisdom and ignorance. Whatever you see, hear, smell, taste, or think, are the phenomena of your subjectivity and objectivity. No matter how subtle or refined these phenomena may be, Zen insists that you cannot attain enlightenment as long as you are the slave of your dualistic attachment.

> Even at the moment of the fatal blow,
> A Zen student keeps his equanimity as usual.
> He carries his meditation moment after moment.
> Nothing in the world can put out his Lamp of Wisdom.
> The sun may turn cold and the moon hot,
> But even then
> No devils or satans can crush
> The ultimate truth of Buddha-Dhamma.
> As the elephant draws the carriage,
> The great wheels are turned.
> Can the road be blocked by a foolish mantis stretching his legs?

A tyrannical king of China once killed a Buddhist monk who refused to marry the royal princess. At the last moment the monk said:

"These groups of four elements have not belonged to me from the beginning. The five *skandhas*[15] deceived you, giving you the illusion of a body. Your sword may as well cut off my head as this spring breeze blows the blossoms from the tree."

Zen offers no miracle to save your life at the last moment, but it can give you equanimity at all times. Just train yourselves in meditation to shut off both your subjectivity and your objectivity. Then you can shut off your subjectivity and melt into your objectivity, or shut off your objectivity and live in your subjectivity. When you can open both your subjectivity and your objectivity, carrying your day's work smoothly and happily, you will be living in Zen. The teaching of Buddha is too simple, so people hesitate to practice it.

The "great-wheels" are Buddha-Dhamma, and the elephant is enlightenment. In China, the mantis has always symbolized a

[15]Skandhas: form (*rupam*); sensation or sense-perception (*vedana*); thought (*samjna*); conformation (*samskara*); consciousness (*vijnana*).

person who overestimates his power. Like a teacher who juggles the ancient names derived from religion and philosophy, seeking to block the road to independent thought, the mantis stretches his legs, but the elephant-drawn carriage rolls on.

> The elephant is not found in the company of rabbits.
> Enlightenment transcends meager intellection.
> Stop looking at the skies through a pipe;
> Heavens exist beyond your measurement.
> There remains nothing but your own actualization.
> Come to me this minute and deal with me personally.

Fragmentary Notes
of Bodhi-Dharma's
Disciples*

Question: What is Buddha-Mind?

Answer: Your mind is it. When you see the selfsame essence of it, you can call it suchness. When you see the changeless nature of it, you can call it Dharma-kaya. It does not belong to anything; therefore, it is called emancipation. It works easily and freely, being never disturbed by others; therefore, it is called the True Path. It was not born, and therefore, it is not going to perish, so it is called Nirvana.

Comment: That mind is not yours. It is a constituent of all sentient beings' minds. You simply call it yours and others' as children play at being grown up.

Question: What is Tathagata?

Answer: One who knows that he comes from nowhere and goes nowhere.

* Early in the twentieth century, M. A. Stein excavated some manuscripts from Tung Huang, among which were notes gathered by Bodhi-Dharma's disciples. These were placed in the National Library of Pei-ping, China, where Dr. D. T. Suzuki copied them, later having them published in Japan in 1933.

Nyogen Senzaki received a copy of the book from which he translated the following notes into English. They consist of a question by a disciple, and the answer by Bodhi-Dharma, and in many cases, a comment by Nyogen Senzaki.

Question: What is Buddha?

Answer: One who realizes the truth and holds nothing that is to be realized.

Comment: Buddha said to Subhuti, "What do you think? In ancient times when the Tathagata was with Dipankara Buddha, did he have attainment in the Dharma?" Subhuti answered, "No, World-honored One, he did not. The Tathagata while with Dipankara Buddha had no attainment whatever in the Dharma." Bodhi-Dharma was certainly the twenty-eighth successor of Buddha Sakyamuni.

Question: What is Dharma?

Answer: It was never produced and will never be reduced; therefore, it is called Dharma, the norm of the universe.

Question: What is *Sangha?*[1]

Answer: It is so named because of the beauty of its harmony.

Comment: We learn nothing but to form a true Sangha . . . harmony of one to another, and harmony of mind and body.

Question: What is meditation in emptiness?

Answer: One observes things in the phenomenal world, yet always dwells in emptiness. That is meditation in emptiness.

Comment: Zengetsu was a descendent of Bodhi-Dharma who lived in China during the Tang Dynasty. As though he wished to illustrate Bodhi-Dharma's words, he said, "Living in the world yet not clinging to nor forming attachments for the dust of the world is the way of the true Zen student." Many Buddhists are like those three monkeys that shut their eyes, ears, and mouths so as not to see, hear, or speak evil. They are afraid to face things in the phenomenal world. Instead of dwelling in emptiness, they build their houses on the sand.

[1] Sangha (Sanskrit): all Buddhists; all priests; Bodhisattvas. Considered one of the three treasures.

Question: How can one dwell in Dharma?

Answer: One should stay neither in in-dwelling Dharma nor in non-dwelling Dharma. One should live naturally in Dharma. This is what you call dwelling in Dharma.

Comment: If you think you are a Zen student, you are labeling yourself unnecessarily. If you call yourself a non-Zen student, you are denying your self and forcing yourself off the path. Just live in Zen naturally beyond all self-recognition. This is what you call dwelling in Dharma.

Question: How can a man live as not-man and a woman as not-woman?

Answer: There is no difference in Buddha-nature between a man and a woman, nor an entity designated as man or woman. Physical matter produces the grass and trees as it does human beings. In comparison you say "grass" or "trees." You give all sorts of names to your illusions. Buddha said, "If one sees that everything exists as an illusion, one can live in a higher sphere than ordinary man."

Comment: Zen is not taking the side of either feminism or misogyny. Both man and woman are Buddha. Only in illusion they appear differently.

Question: If one attains the Nirvana of an arhat, has he Zen realization?

Answer: He is just dreaming and so are you.

Comment: Just like Bodhi-Dharma! Did you hear what he said?

Question: If one practices the six paramitas, and passes through the ten stages of Bodhisattvahood, and completes ten thousand virtues, he should know that all things are not born; therefore, they are not going to perish. Such realization is neither intuition nor intellectuality. He has nothing to receive and there is nothing to receive him. Has this man Zen realization?

Answer: He is just dreaming and so are you.

Question: If a man has ten powers, accomplishes four forms of fearlessness, and completes eighteen systems of the teaching, he is the same as Buddha who attained enlightenment under the pipala tree. He can save all sentient beings and then enter into Nirvana. Is he not a real Buddha?

Answer: He is just dreaming and so are you.

Question: I have heard that all Buddhas in the past, present, and future preach the same Dharma, and that countless beings are saved from suffering. Is it not true?

Answer: You have heard someone speak of dreams, and you yourself are actually dreaming. Whatever you figure with your dualistic mind never makes a true account of Mind-Essence, therefore, I call you a dreamer. Dream is one thing and realization another. Do not mix them together. Wisdom in the dream is not the real wisdom. One who has true wisdom does not hold self-recognition. Buddhas in the past, present, and future are in the realm beyond cognition. If you shut off your thinking faculty, blocking off the road of your mind, you will enter a different sphere. Until that time, whatever you think, whatever you say, whatever you do is nothing but foolishness in dreamland.

Comment: What are the six paramitas? What are the ten stages of Bodhisattvahood? What are the ten thousand virtues? What are the ten powers? What are the four forms of fearlessness? What are the eighteen systems of teaching? When you travel by plane do you recite the name of each city, town, or whistle-stop over which you pass? Zen demands that you start without hesitation, proceeding to your destination quickly and directly. Bodhi-Dharma is calling you. Why don't you wake up!

Question: What kind of wisdom should one use to cut off delusions?

Answer: When you observe your delusions, you will know that they are baseless and not dependable. In this way you can cut confusion and doubt. This is what I call wisdom.

Comment: A Zen student should not fear delusions. He should gaze at them squarely and determine their true nature. A Japanese poem says, "The real form of the ghost was nothing but a group of withered reeds in the late autumn field."

Question: What sort of delusions will be cleared by Zen?
Answer: Any delusions of mediocrity, of a philosopher, of a Çravaka, of a Pratyeka-Buddha, or of a Bodhisattva.
Comment: Bodhi-Dharma thinks that all these people should wash their faces in the cold water of Zen.

Question: What is the difference between a sage's most excellent life and the common people's everyday life?
Answer: It is like gossamer. Some mistake it for vapor, but it is in fact a spider's silk that floats in the air. A mediocre person sees the sage's life, and believes it to be the same as his own everyday life; whereas the enlightened man sees the holy path in a life of mediocrity. You will observe in the Sutras that all Buddhas preach for two groups . . . the mediocre and the wise, but in the eye of Zen, a sage's life is one of mediocrity and the mediocre person's is the sage's. This one life has no form and is empty by nature. If you become attached to any form, you should reject it. If you see an ego, a soul, a birth, or a death, reject them all.

Question: Why and how do we reject them?
Answer: If you have Zen, you should not see a thing. The *Tao-Teh-Ching* says, "The most firmly established in the path appears the most remiss."
Comment: Zen is the offspring of Buddhism and Taoism. Bodhi-Dharma refers to the forty-first section of the *Tao-Teh-Ching*: "The superior man, as soon as he hears of the path, earnestly practices the teaching; the average man, hearing of the path, sometimes remembers it and sometimes forgets it; the inferior man, hearing of the path, ridicules it. The teaching of the path

resembles a deep valley; the most innocent appears to be most ashamed; the highest of virtues appears to be the humblest; the most firmly established in the path appears the most remiss; the finest instrument is the latest to be perfected; the largest bell sounds rarely. The path is unseen and inscrutable; nevertheless, it is precisely this path alone that can give and accomplish."

Question: What do you call the mind of greediness?
Answer: It is the mind of ignorance.

Question: What do you call the mind of egolessness?
Answer: It is the mind of Çravaka, Buddha's actual disciple.

Question: What do you call the mind of no-entity?
Answer: It is the mind of sages who have no connection with the teaching of Buddha, but discover the truth of no-entity by themselves.

Question: What do you call the mind that has no particular understanding and also no painful delusions?
Answer: It is the mind of Bodhisattvas.

Question: What do you call the mind that has nothing to know and also nothing to realize?
Answer: No answer from Bodhi-Dharma.
Comment: Bodhi-Dharma once said, "Dharma-kaya has no form, therefore, one sees it without seeing. Dharma has no voice; therefore, one hears it without hearing. Prajna has nothing to be known; therefore, one knows it without knowing. If a person thinks that he is seeing, he sees it incompletely. If he thinks that he knows it, he does not know it thoroughly. When he knows it without knowing, he knows it completely. If one does not know this, he is not a true knower. If one thinks that he is gaining, he is not gaining entirely. When he gains non-gaining, he owns

everything. If one thinks that he is right, his righteousness is not perfect. When he transcends right and wrong, his virtues are accomplished. Such wisdom is the gate-opener to a hundred thousand gates of the higher wisdom."

Although these recorded teachings of Bodhi-Dharma were lost in the caves of Tung Huang for more than thirteen hundred years, Zen students continued to live as he taught. The Lamp of Dharma still burns, proving that wisdom itself is untransmissible and only to be obtained by living.

There is a Zen poem written by a remote descendent of Bodhi-Dharma:

> When the soft rain moistens my clothes,
> I see the Buddha without seeing.
> When a petal of a flower falls quietly,
> I hear the voice of the Patriarch without hearing.

"See Dharma-kaya without seeing." Dharma-kaya is nothing but your own true self, if I express it ethically. As a religious term it is called "Buddha-kaya," and philosophically, "Dharma-kaya." Hakuin says, "It is the sound of one hand," and this wandering monk in America declares it is the single eye of which Meister Eckhart has spoken. Never mind the names! It is neither knowable nor unknowable. Just see it without seeing, hear it without hearing, and gain it without gaining. Bodhi-Dharma mentions the hundred thousand gates of wisdom. Do not count them. If you do, you will be imprisoned. Tell your great-great-grandfather they are all gateless gates in dreamland.

Said Bodhi-Dharma, "All Buddhas preach emptiness. Why? Because they wish to crush the concrete ideas of the students. If a student even clings to an idea of emptiness, he betrays all Buddhas. One clings to life although there is nothing to be called life; another clings to death although there is nothing to be called death. In reality there is nothing to be born, consequently, there is nothing to perish.

"By clinging, one recognizes a thing or an idea. Reality has no inside, outside, nor middle part. An ignorant person creates delusions and suffers from discrimination. Right and wrong do not exist in reality. An ignorant person creates them, recognizes them, near or far, inward or outward. He then suffers from discrimination. This is the general way of the phenomenal world."

Comment: When I was a child, my foster father gave me my first lesson in emptiness. He used to keep all sweets in a box, passing it to me occasionally when I would ask him if there was anything in it. One day he answered, "This time there is nothing but emptiness." "May I please have that emptiness?" I asked. My foster father answered, "My dear child, emptiness has no form, no color. It has no sound, no odor. You cannot taste it in your mouth. You cannot touch it with your hand. It did not enter this box, and it will not go out of the box. It is neither good nor bad. It is neither pretty nor ugly. It is neither heavy nor light. I know that you will neither like it nor dislike it. Now look and see!" He then took off the cover of the box. At the time I knew only that there was no sweet in the box; the meaning of his words was beyond my comprehension. It took me more than ten years of study and Zen meditation to realize the true meaning of emptiness. The words of Bodhi-Dharma may not be clear to you, but be patient and wait until you actually experience it. These words hold the brilliancy of the Lamp of Dharma. I hope that you will devote yourselves to constant meditation and discover the light that will illumine not only yourselves, but all sentient beings in the world.

Bodhi-Dharma said to his disciples, "The teaching of Buddha gives you the highest wisdom. No one can describe it without experience. For generation after generation all patriarchs worked hard for it. None of them wasted time for foolish things. They practiced what the ordinary man cannot practice. They bore what the common people cannot bear. If you have some virtues and knowledge of the world, do not be conceited about them.

With such petty attainment how can you turn the wheel of Dharma of the Mahayana teaching?"

If you American students carry the spirit of this saying, you need not depend upon the trash excavated at Tung Huang. Just go straight ahead to the palace of your own innerliness and meet the Blue-eyed Monk face to face.

Question: Are there fast and slow ways of attainment?
Answer: If one sees that endless time is the mind, he will attain quickly, but if he makes a point in his mind and aims at his destination, he will attain slowly. The wise one knows that his mind is the path; the stupid one makes a path beyond his mind. He does not know where the path is nor does he know that mind itself is the path.
Comment: Whoever recorded these sayings of Bodhi-Dharma must have had slow reaction time. For present American students the first two sentences are more than enough. One does not punch a time clock twice upon arrival.

Question: Why does one attain quickly?
Answer: Because mind is the body of the path, and therefore is quickly reached. Stupid ones mark their own time, starting according to that standard; therefore, they must make their own destination according to their own delusions.
Comment: For instance, if one wants to enjoy life, one can do it wherever and whenever desired. If he aims at something to be acquired, he must create his own destination using his concept of time and place. With the addition of two more delusions, he cannot enjoy his life thoroughly.

Question: What part of the mind is the body of the path?
Answer: Mind is like the wood or stone from which a person carves an image. If he carves a dragon or a tiger, and upon seeing

it fears it, he is like a stupid person creating a picture of hell and then afraid to face it. If he does not fear it, then his unnecessary thoughts will vanish. Part of the mind produces sight, sound, taste, odor, and sensibility, and from them raises greed, anger, and ignorance with all their accompanying likes and dislikes. Thus is planted the seed, which grows to great suffering. If one realizes from the beginning that Mind-Essence is empty and quiet, he should know no specific time or place. Instead, he makes an image of a tiger, lion, dragon, demon, warrior, or other monster, recognizes them by comparison, and produces likes and dislikes. If he knows that from the beginning there is no such thing, then he should know that Mind-Essence is not formed; therefore, these images are nothing but illusions. When he realizes this fact, he will be emancipated at that instant.

Question: What is the natural, simple mind, and what is the artificial, complicated mind?
Answer: Letters and speeches come from the artificial, complicated mind. Both in the material and immaterial world a person stays or goes, sits or lies down, and moves innocently, or, it can be said, in the natural, simple mind. When one remains unmoved by pleasure or suffering, his mind may be called the natural, simple mind.

Question: What is right and what is wrong?
Answer: Discrimination with no-mind is right. Discrimination with mind is wrong. When one transcends right and wrong, he is truly right. In a Sutra it says, "When one dwells on the right road, one does not discriminate, 'this is right, this is wrong.'"
Comment: "With mind" means with self-centered, psychological movement. "With no-mind" means unhampered, natural, selfless movement.

Question: What is a sagacious student, and what is a dull student?
Answer: A sagacious student does not depend on his teacher's words, but uses his own experience to find the truth. A dull student depends on coming to a gradual understanding through his teacher's words. A teacher has two kinds of students: one hears the teacher's words without clinging to the material nor to the immaterial, without attaching to form or to non-form, without thinking of animate objects or of inanimate objects . . . this is the sagacious student; the other, who is avid for understanding, accumulates meanings, and mixes good and bad, is the dull student. The sagacious student understands instantly; he does not raise inferior mind when he hears the teaching, nor does he follow the sage's mind. Instead, he transcends both wisdom and ignorance. Even though a person hears the teaching and does not cling to worldly desires, and does not love Buddha or the true path, if, when he has to select one out of two, he selects quietness from confusion, wisdom from ignorance, inactivity from activity, and clings to one or the other of these, then he is a dull student. If one transcends both wisdom and ignorance, has no greed for the teaching, does not live in right recollectedness, does not raise right thinking, and does not have aspirations to be Pratyeka-Buddha nor Bodhisattva, then he is a sagacious student.

Suggestions for Zen Students

BY ZENGETSU*

Living in the world, yet not clinging to or forming attachments for the dust of the world, is the way of a true Zen student.

In witnessing the good actions of another person, encourage yourself to follow his example. In hearing of the mistaken action of another person, advise yourself not to emulate it.

Even though you are alone in a dark room, conduct yourself as though you were facing a noble guest.

Express your feelings, but never become more expressive than your true nature.

Poverty is your treasure. Do not exchange it for an easy life.

A person may look like a fool and yet not be stupid. He may be conserving his wisdom and guarding it carefully.

The virtues are the fruits of self-discipline, and do not drop from heaven of themselves like rain or hail.

Modesty is the foundation of all virtues. Let your neighbors find you before you make yourself known to them.

A noble heart never forces itself forward. Its words are as rare gems seldom displayed.

* The biography of Zengetsu is unknown except that he was a student of Tokusan (782–865 A.D.) and Sekiso (807–888 A.D.).

Every day is a fortunate day for a true student. Time passes but he never lags behind.

Neither glory nor shame can move his heart.

Do not discuss right or wrong. Always censure yourself, never another.

Some things, although right, were considered wrong for many generations. Since the value of righteousness may be recognized after centuries, there is no need to crave immediate appreciation.

Why do you not leave everything to the great law of the universe and pass each day with a peaceful smile?

Glossary

Asamskrita: not subject to causation; the world of birthlessness and deathlessness.

Avalokitesvara: the Buddha of Compassion; in Chinese *Kwan-yin*; in Japanese *Kwannon*.

Bodhisattva: a person dedicated not only to his own enlightenment but also to the enlightenment of all sentient beings and in this way distinct from *Ahrat*.

Buddha-Dhamma (Pali; Buddha-Dharma in Sanskrit): enlightened wisdom.

Buddha-hrydaya: brilliancy of enlightenment.

Buddha Sakyamuni: the same as Gautama Buddha.

Çravaka (Sanskrit): the four noble truths.

Dharma (Sanskrit; Dhamma in Pali): the content of enlightenment to be realized intuitively, directly, and personally experienced.

Dharma-kaya: same as Dharma-body; the Law body of the Buddha; original man in full; the sound of one hand; the eternal Buddha.

Dhyana (Sanskrit): meditation.

Dipankara Buddha: one of the early Buddhas before the time of Gautama Buddha.

Hinayana: Small Vehicle, one of the two main groups of Buddhists.

Karma: the law of cause and effect.

Koan: a problem given to a student for solution.

Maha-Kasyapa: a disciple of Buddha and first to receive the Lamp of Dharma, which was later transmitted in a direct line through Bodhi-Dharma, the patriarchs, etc.

Mahayana: Great Vehicle, one of the two main groups of Buddhists.

Mahaprajna (Sanskrit): great wisdom, the wisdom of the Buddhas.

Nidana: process of karma relation.

Nirvana: synonymous with enlightenment, but is not the negative condition as translated by many scholars, nor is it a condition of non-
existence to be found outside of Samsara.

Paramitas (Sanskrit): the six noble deeds; facets of Buddha-nature.

Prajna: that condition of the ability to see directly into the true nature of
things beyond mere intellection.

Prajnaparamita: the Sixth Precept, or practice of wisdom.

Samadhi: is sometimes used in place of dhyana, but more often is referred to as that condition achieved by the practice of dhyana.

Samatha: quietude.

Samsara: world of birth and death.

Samskrita: subject to causation; the world of birth and death.

Sangha (Sanskrit): all Buddhists; all priests; Bodhisattvas considered one
of the three treasures.

Sanzen (from Chinese *San-Ch'an*): to study Zen, especially the examination of a student by a teacher.

Sastras or Shastras: commentaries on the Sutras.

Skandhas: form (*rupam*); sensation or sense-perception (*vedana*);
thought (*samjna*); conformation (*samskara*); consciousness
(*vijnana*).

Sutra (Sanskrit): the portion of the Tripitaka containing the teachings of
Buddha.

Tathagata: Buddha; Mind-Essence; Eternal Presence; Eternal Now.

Tathagata-dhyana: enlightened meditation.

Tripitaka: literally, "Three Baskets." All the Buddhist scriptures as a unit.

Vipassana: contemplation or discernment (Tendai School).

Zazen (from the Chinese *tso ch'an*): to sit in meditation.

A Bibliography of Books
by Nyogen Senzaki
and Books Containing
His Writings

Buddha and His Disciples (A Guide to Buddhism), by Kōken Murano
(Tokyo: Sanyusha, 1932).
> Contains Sōen Shaku's "The First Step in Meditation," a foreword by
> Nyogen Senzaki, forty stories by Murano, and a supplement with nine
> essays and talks by Senzaki.

The Gateless Gate: Transcribed from the Chinese by Nyogen Senzaki and
Saladin Reps (Los Angeles: John Murray, 1934).
> The first English translation of the *Wu-mên kuan (Mumonkan)*.

Ten Bulls: A Chinese Classic, transcribed by Nyogen Senzaki and Saladin Reps (Los Angeles: DeVorss, 1935; reprinted, Portland, Oregon:
Ralph R. Phillips, c. 1946).
> "The Ten Oxherding Pictures," with a translation of the traditional
> commentary. Reprint not examined, not in Library of Congress.

On Zen Meditation: What a Buddhist Monk in America Said, by Nyogen Senzaki, Note by Nanshin Okamoto (Kyoto: Bukkasha, 1936).
> Includes Senzaki's essays found in *The Buddha and His Disciples* ex-
> cept "The Mealtime Ceremony in the Buddhist Monastery," plus
> eleven others.

What American Buddhist Pioneers Think, compiled by Kōken Murano
(Japan, 1939).
> Lectures and essays by Senzaki. Not examined.

101 Zen Stories, transcribed by Nyogen Senzaki and Paul Reps (London: Rider and Philadelphia: David McKay, 1940).

From the Chinese and Japanese Zen traditions.

Zen Flesh, Zen Bones: A Collection of Zen and Pre-Zen Writings, compiled by Paul Reps (Rutland, Vt.: Tuttle, 1957, 1970).

A collection of *The Gateless Gate*, *101 Bulls*, and *101 Zen Stories*, with a Yogic treatise titled "Centering."

The Iron Flute: One Hundred Zen Kōan with Commentary by Genrō, Fūgai, and Nyogen, translated and edited by Nyogen Senzaki and Ruth Strout McCandless, illustrated by Toriichi Murashima (Rutland, Vt.: Tuttle, 1964, 1985).

A translation of *Tetteki Tōsui*, a nineteenth-century Japanese collection of classic Chinese and a few Indian Zen cases, with commentaries.

Namu Dai Bosa: A Transmission of Zen Buddhism to America by Nyogen Senzaki, Soen Nakagawa, Eido Shimano, edited with an introduction by Louis Nordstrom (New York: Theatre Arts Books, 1976).

Includes biographical information, poems and thirty essays by Senzaki, photographs.

Like a Dream, Like a Fantasy: The Zen Writings of Nyogen Senzaki, Eido Shimano, edited by (Tokyo: Japan Publications, 1978).

Talks, essays, translations, and poems.

Sattmann (replacement)